# Just Call Me Jock

## Tom Murphy

Barb's Beer Foundation, publisher

Published by
Barb's Beer Foundation
1711 Elllis St., Suite 201
Bellingham, WA 98225
tom@tommurphy.com
barbsbeer.org

The Library of Congress Cataloging-in-Publication Data Applied For

Tom Murphy
Just Call Me Jock

p.      cm
ISBN 978-0-9983712-0-7
1. Sports   2. Running   3. Biography   I. Title
2017

Printed in the United States of America

1 3 5 7 9 10 8 6 4 2

Book design by White Horse Enterprises, Inc.

For interviews or information regarding special discounts for bulk
purchases, please contact Tom Murphy at tom@tommurphy.com

## Other books by Tom Murphy

*Just Call Me Jock* (1982)
*Reclaiming the Sky*

## Dedication

For Jock, Johnny, Caitlin, Justin, Peggy, Johanne, Terry—and Barb. Great runners in the "race," all!

## About Jock Semple: From Legends and Experts

"Jock gave the world one of the most galvanizing photos in the women's rights movement! 'The Great Shove' on the Boston course in 1967 was the spark that ignited the women's running revolution. Jock was a complex mix of irascible, funny, hot-tempered and lovable. He changed my life in an instant and as a consequence he changed millions of women's lives."
—Kathrine Switzer, first woman to finish the Boston Marathon wearing an official bib number, eight-time runner of the Boston Marathon (PR 2:51), founder of the 261 Fearless movement and author of *Marathon Woman*.

"The first time I walked into Jock's Boston Garden clinic I felt I had stepped back in time into a world peopled by Clarence DeMar, Jim Peters, the two Johnny Kelleys. and all the others who had made the Boston Marathon great."
—Bill Rodgers, four-time winner of the Boston and New York Marathons. In the early 1970s Bill ran for Jock's Boston Athletic Association team.

"At the 1972 Boston Marathon, Jock waved us over to start with the men. He was always friendly and supportive and that meant so much to us."
—Nina Kuscsik, winner of the 1972 Boston Marathon women's division, the first year women were formally permitted to compete with men.

"Jock Semple was always true to his principles."

—Jacqueline Gareau, official winner of the 1980 Boston Marathon (the year Rosie Ruiz, an imposter, jumped in and crossed the finish line first. As Rosie was "crowned" it was Jock who led the protests to affirm Jackie as the true winner).

"During the early to mid 1980s there was real concern whether the Boston Marathon would survive. Some camps wanted us to keep the marathon an amateur race, others wanted us to embrace modernity with all the changes that would entail, from accepting sponsors to giving prize money and more.

I give Jock Semple great credit for his sage advice that helped me understand the fundamental values of the race, values my new team needed to affirm. Each morning during those early days I would walk from Boston Garden to the Park Plaza Hotel for meetings, and beside me walked Jock. He was eighty-two at that point, but as spry as ever. With each step he imparted insights formed during his more than fifty-year involvement with the race, and I remember his words, 'Change can come, but never compromise the integrity of the Boston Marathon. Keep this a race for the runners, always.'

That we tried to do with every decision, every day, and thanks to Jock who saw the path clear, that's the path that worked then and preserves the character today and always will."

—Guy Morse, B.A.A. Executive Director (retired.) Guy headed up the Boston Marathon for twenty-eight years (1985–2012), and took the helm during a tenuous time. He provided inspired, professional leadership that helped the Boston Marathon grow increasingly as a world class event.

"As a medical student in Boston, I used to love watching the Boston Marathon. I'm grateful that this book is being republished now to support efforts to *find a cure for lung cancer*."

—Dr. Howard West, founder of cancerGRACE.org and one of America's leading experts who is working to cure lung cancer, a cancer that claims the lives of more women each year than any other cancer.

"From the Great Depression through the 1960s, Jock was *the* force, not only in Boston, but in all of New England running."

—Tom Derderian, executive producer, Boston Marathon Documentary

# Foreword

## The Starting Gun!

THINGS ARE EPHEMERAL, MEMORIES sustain us.

Here's a favorite memory of mine from 1980. I was an aspiring young writer working for $36.50 a day as a substitute teacher in the Boston public school system when Jock Semple asked me to write his life story. Jock, of course, was the famous Scottish-American marathon runner. In addition, he was a physical therapist for the Boston Bruins and the Boston Celtics, an Olympic trainer, and a sports official who was also the co-director of the Boston Marathon.

Jock was a legend in the running world, so naturally, I jumped at the chance. Every afternoon after school I sat in Jock's "Salon de Rubdown," his training cubicle in the huge sports arena known as the Boston Garden, and absorbed Jock's amazing stories about the early days of running, Boston Marathon lore and pungent lineament fumes.

As winter turned to spring a theme emerged: "Johnny this, Johnny that." Jock repeatedly said the words as he recounted the evolution of the Boston Marathon from dusty dirt roads to what, by the 1980s, was becoming a pathway to gold. The 1980s were the running boom days, and I scribbled furiously in my notepad as Jock spoke. (No digital iPads in those days!)

"Johnny was the finest pure marathon runner I had ever seen," Jock said, as he performed rubdowns on his clients and talked to me over his shoulder, "but he came along in the 1950s, too early for acclaim."

And so the journalist in me realized I had not just a sports memoir at hand, but possibly a wonderful "father-son type story" as well. I knew I had to find "Johnny," whose full name was John J. Kelley. In running circles in Boston, however, he was known as "Johnny the Younger" to distinguish him from John A. Kelley, or "Johnny the Elder," a running colleague of Jock's from the thirties and forties. I just felt I had to invite Johnny the Younger to join Jock's and my book project.

Another enduring memory from that period, this one from the 1980 Boston Marathon Expo in the Hynes Convention Center. The expo is *the* place to look for new running gear, the latest technologies, and other running products and services during marathon week.

It was evening, and the expo was about to close when I spotted a tiny curly headed fellow. He had a Bobby Kennedy profile and was surrounded by a crowd who peppered the tiny fellow with questions about his 1957 Boston Marathon win. This man, I surmised, was Johnny Kelley the Younger. My research had shown that he also was a second place finisher in the Boston Marathon five times, a two-time Olympian (1956 and 1960,) a Pan American Games Marathon winner, and an eight times American National Marathon champion. This last amazing feat is one that has never been duplicated.

In a soft voice, Johnny answered every question, even though many were redundant, and his big, welcoming smile never flagged.

I made eye contact with a lady beside him, a woman I later came to find was his wife, Jessie. "Johnny," she said as a break occurred in the constant flow of questions, "you have someone waiting to talk to you."

Johnny flashed me a blue-eyed grin indicating that he'd be with me in a moment. While I waited, I saw that he never cut anyone short and I was becoming witness to the special gift Johnny Kelley possessed, the trait that endeared him to the legions who knew and revered him: - the way Johnny Kelley treated *everyone* as special.

Johnny eventually became my co-author on the first edition of *Just Call Me Jock*. Sadly, Johnny passed away in 2011 at age eighty, but his essence remains in this updated, second edition of the book. Even though Johnny has passed, he remains vivid in my memory for two reasons: first for the wondrous experience we had working together to bring Jock's story to life, and second, for the enduring friendship I forged with him during that process.

I'm sure Jock, who passed away at age eighty-four in 1988, would want Johnny's contribution to be acknowledged in this edition of the book as well. Not just because he was the finest runner of his era, but also because he was a man who was regarded by all who knew him as one of the kindest, most decent people who ever lived.

If you ever get a chance to pass through Mystic, Connecticut, do yourself a favor and take time to stop to look at the statue of Johnny Kelley, which was created by Jim Roy and a legion of townspeople. Don't worry about directions. Just say the "Johnny Kelley statue," and you'll be sent in the right direction without hesitation. Everyone in Mystic knows Johnny Kelley!

Now onto the early days of running that Jock Semple shared in the first edition of this book which was initially published in

1982. Now, in 2017, the second edition is being published through the Barb's Beer Foundation, which I'll explain in a moment. Ironically, the publication of this edition coincides with the fiftieth anniversary of an unusual event that made Jock famous, or should I say, "infamous."

Many people know the story about Jock chasing runner Kathrine Switzer down the road in the 1967 Boston Marathon to get "his" number back. I say "his" number, because that's how Jock saw it when, after assigning Kathrine an official Boston Marathon number (261) by "mistake," he took it upon himself to rectify the error and gave chase to protect the sanctity of the rules, which prohibited women from entering or running in the competition.

As a result of the Jock and Kathrine chase, people somehow got the idea that Jock was against women. In truth, he later became a strong supporter of the women's running movement, which he (inadvertently) helped to usher in. Jock also became great friends with Kathrine. Later, you'll see a photo of Jock giving her a hug, and that in itself shows the depth of change in this man. So I urge you, those who never met Jock and who may be horrified by the 1967 incident, to keep an open mind.

All of that is in the book, or in "my boooook," as Jock used to call it, and we hope that the Kathrine Switzer story, along with many other stories will reintroduce one of Boston's most colorful sports figures to a new generation of readers and running enthusiasts. After the horror of the bombing at the 2013 marathon, we offer these stories from the early days of the sport of running, and from the race's early days, as another step also in the continuous process of healing.

One more personal memory, and that is of watching my wife, Barb, cross the finish line at the 2000 Boston Marathon. That was a feat she desperately wanted to accomplish before her fiftieth birthday—and she did. Barb and I ran many marathons together during our thirty-three-year marriage, but for a girl born and raised in Boston, running the Boston Marathon was a great source of pride.

Several years later, Barb was diagnosed with non-smoker's lung cancer. She fought the disease for six years before she passed away in December of 2013. As a runner, and as a person, Barb was all about action, and during her illness she worked hard to create awareness for the disease, which is on the rise, especially among women.

After Barb passed away, when we were looking for a way to continue her proactive mantle, we created Barb's Beer along with a promotional campaign called "Racing to the Cure." There were a great many of us who wanted to continue her fight in her name.

Our goal with Barb's Beer and the Barb's Beer Foundation that supports the cause, is to raise funds to assist the efforts of Barb's oncologist, Dr. Howard West, who is one of the country's leading cancer experts. He is also the founder of a charity, cancer-GRACE.org, that is working diligently to find that cure.

You'll see more about Barb's Beer and our Racing to the Cure campaign in the back of the book, but I'll conclude with two points. First, all of my author proceeds will go to the Barb's Beer Foundation. Second, you may be interested to know that the logo for Barb's Beer is a silhouette of Barb crossing the finish line at the 2000 Boston Marathon. She kept the photo to savor the memory, and I can tell you that even though she has passed on, I know she will savor the moment when Dr. West and his colleagues find a cure that insures no one else ever gets non smoker's lung cancer.

Now onto *Just Call Me Jock*, which opens with an introduction from Amby Burfoot, editor-at-large for *Runner's World*, and to my mind the finest writer on running of our generation. Amby, whose latest book is *First Ladies of Running*, also offers an epilogue at the end of this new edition that addresses the tremendous growth in women's running precipitated, to a large extent, by Jock's jaunt down the road in 1967. I thank him, Gloria Ratti, Kathrine Switzer, Billy Rodgers and so many others in the Boston running community for all their support.

Most of all, I thank you for taking this "run through time" with Johnny, Jock and me, anew.

Tom Murphy
April, 2017

# Introduction

TO TELL THE TRUTH, I can't actually remember the first time I met
Jock Semple. In New England road racing circles, you see, the legend preceded the man. As a teenager first testing myself on the
roads in the early 1960s, I heard Jock stories everywhere. The best—
—the most intimate and improbable—were recounted by members
of his beloved Boston Athletic Association (BAA) running club.
(Did one of them really tell me that on a six-hundred-mile drive
into Canada Jock once stopped, worried about a worn front tire,
to patch the balding rubber with athletic tape?) But you didn't have
to belong to the BAA to know Jock. He considered no man beyond
his purview and was famous for his last minute, locker room
sweeps: "Awright, all you bums and laggards, get outta here. The
gun goes off in five minutes."

From there he took to the roads himself. Usually he would
drive the course in some behemoth vehicle, and a good thing too,
as these were not only pre-gas crunch days but pre-running boom
as well. Jock functioned as pace car, police force, water stop, and
coach. An indelible image: I am running a Sunday road race, mid
1960s, in one of the countless towns ringing Boston, perhaps Jock's
own town of Lynn. It is a ten-mile race, in July, and after six miles

everyone is beginning to flag. I am struggling to stay up with Ken Mueller, a BAA member; we're in the bottom half of the race's top ten. The scenery, alternating used car lots, furniture warehouses, and bars, does not inspire. Occasionally we veer out from the curbside to avoid a broken beer bottle.

The sound of our heaving breath is broken by a car squealing around a corner. Tiredly, we turn our heads. Jock is zooming up behind us. He is driving with his right arm, while the rest of his body is leaning far out the front window, turned backward, the better to inspect the long line of runners and count positions. Though he cannot see ahead, the pressure on the accelerator remains constant. In a moment he has passed us, stopped the car, and raced across the street with cups of water. "C'mon Muuuer," he screams at Ken, "Millrose is coming up behind you. We need your place. Don't lose it."

He storms back to the car, more red-faced than we are, and punches it hard up the road, hoping to find a BAA runner out ahead of the lead pack. Two miles farther down the road the same scene repeats itself.

Jock Semple is, of course, a man meant to be heard. The typewriter can never do justice to the fusillade of fiery words, the inflections, the old world metaphors. One time before the Boston Marathon, when I visited Jock in his Boston Garden training room, he picked up one of the daily dozens of pre-marathon phone calls.

"Hello," he growled into the receiver. Then, after a brief pause to listen: "I'm the stooge does all the work. Whaddaya want?"

But my favorite Jock outburst took place at a classy New York press conference, proving that he did not temper himself to the social strata. This was a press conference hosted by Avon, the women's cosmetics firm, and organized by Kathrine Switzer.

Switzer, you'll recall, I s the woman who made Jock (in)famous, and vice versa when he attempted to bully her off the Boston Marathon course in 1967 because the Amateur Athletic Union (AAU) did not then permit women to run marathons.

"I didn't have anything against her," Jock always insisted, "but I was always taught to uphold rules and regulations."

Anyway, he and Kathrine had long since made their peace by the time of the Avon press conference and she shrewdly invited him, because during the event she announced the formation of the Avon Women's Running Circuit. After introducing Jock and other invited guests, Switzer outlined the organization of the running circuit, and then opened the floor to questions from reporters.

Someone immediately asked what she would do if a man tried to enter one of the women-only races. Jock, who had been seated up front, was on his feet and crimson before Switzer had a chance to answer. Turning and almost accusing the questioner, he raged, "No good runner would ever do that. And I'd call him a schmuck. I can't spell it but that's a Jewish word meaning a bum, a joker, a tramp, a no good."

Of course, Jock's story is inevitably intertwined with the Boston Marathon, and well I remember the first years I ran Boston. With fields numbering under a thousand, we didn't need elaborate seeding arrangements. There was no National Guard, no roped off sections, no mile time placards. Jock took care of everything. His only equipment was a burly shoulder. If you wore a high number, you didn't dare edge forward. If you had a BAA unicorn logo on your racing jersey, Jock found a place for you in the second or third row, even if you weren't one of the swiftest. It was, after all, the BAA Marathon.

Just before the gun, Jock would disappear into the press bus, and I wouldn't see him until after the race. Until one April day in

1968, that is, when I led the pack over Heartbreak Hill and found the press bus mere yards ahead as we began to descend toward the Prudential Center in Boston. Moments like that you don't forget. Nor will I ever forget the sight of the portly Scotsman (he later slimmed down) forcing two thirds of his body out a rear window and yelling, "Give it hell down the hill, Aaamby, give it hell down the hill." I did, and it made all the difference.

Sometimes I find it difficult to separate Jock, the man and the athlete, from Jock, the source of countless uproarious stories. But then I remember the framed Boston Marathon certificate hanging in his office (the certificate notes his seventh place finish in 2:44:29 in the 1930 Boston Marathon), and I remind myself that these certificates were an innovation of the 1970s. I understood that he was a proud runner, like the rest of us. I remember, too, that I almost never had a conversation with Jock in which he failed to mention the two running clubs of his life: the Clydesdale Harriers (of Scotland), and the BAA. If he was not talking about Bill Rodgers or Patti Catalano, both of whom cut their road racing teeth with the BAA, he was waxing enthusiastic over a high schooler, or perhaps the club's crack Masters squad.

In the end, though, what I valued most about Jock was his purely emotional character. In this age of plastic men formed sometimes by Madison Avenue, sometimes by the contradictory forces of life, Jock remained cast in an original and unchanging mold. He could never be packaged. He did not recite lines from a teleprompter. His reactions sprung from instinct and were expressed with a sputter and an instant opinion. While others debated the Rosie Ruiz case, Jock instantly declared, "She's a fraud and a phony."

Rosie Ruiz, of course, was the runner who was declared the winner in the female category of the 84th Boston Marathon in

1980, only to have her title stripped eight days later when it was discovered that she had not run the entire course.

Jock Semple was incapable of—did not know—the ways of vacillation, disingenuousness, or putting on airs. You never had to guess where he stood. Despite the Boston Marathon's strict qualifying standards (that he staunchly defended), despite stories of bullying and club favoritism (that I have here added to), Jock was far from being an elitist. He remained true to his own working class roots and working class introduction to athletics. All he asked was that you devote yourself to sport and honor, as he did.

The afternoon before one Boston Marathon, as he shepherded over tables where runners were picking up their numbers. Jock complained to me, "Oh Amby, my schedule is terrible. I've got to be here all afternoon, and then over to the Garden at five for the Bruins, and then back here tomorrow morning at five to lead everyone onto the buses. I don't know how much longer I can keep this up."

A tough schedule, true. Bone-wearying. But I didn't find myself feeling sorry for Jock. I knew a lament of love when I heard one.

Amby Burfoot
Editor at large, *Runner's World*, and 1968 Boston Marathon winner

# Chapter One

## Jock: The Baron of Glasgow

IT'S 6:10 A.M. AND the sun cast its first vermilion splash over dusty Boston Garden as an old man shuffles up the worn terrazzo stairs to his tiny physiotherapy clinic. Wearing a cotton jacket over his t-shirt and white baggy pants, the old man once pushed a broom in a dingy factory in Scotland before becoming a great marathon runner, trainer, and co-director of the Boston Marathon. He turns the key in a chipped, steel-plated door marked J.D. SEMPLE.

Inside he removes his coat and hangs it on a hook where the cinder block walls of his cramped cubicle seep liniment fumes. Photos of great moments in the Boston Marathon curl inside their sixty-nine cent Woolworth frames as he switches on the fan, diathermy machine (a device that provides heat to a specific part of the body in high-frequency electric currents), and the hot box. Then he clears his desk with his forearm before glancing down at a mousetrap behind the door. The trap still sports the cheese, and he smiles to see that the Celtics' cat has been doing its job.

The old man puts new soap in the shower stall, then cuts the string on a tall stack of towels to finish prepping his clinic for his "patients," as he calls the athletes and assorted businessmen who will begin to arrive soon.

Nearly eighty years old, Jock Semple continues to work six days a week, attending to patients in his "Salon de Rubdown," as Boston sportswriters Leo Monahan and Tim Horgan have dubbed his Boston Garden clinic.

"I've gotten lazy," he once told Monahan. "For twenty-five years I worked in my clinic seven days a week. Now I take Wednesdays off. That is, when I don't come in."

Above his desk, which is laden with Boston Marathon mail, hangs a plaque from the legendary Boston Bruins hockey star Bobby Orr (one of his favorite patients). It reads: TO JOCK: A GUY WHO HAS SO MANY FRIENDS BECAUSE HE RUBS EVERYBODY THE RIGHT WAY."

Jock administered to athletes in a dozen sports over three decades. His skilled hands kneaded many great names, including Bobby Orr, and Celtic stars Bob Cousy, Bill Russell, Jack Dempsey, Rocky Marciano, John Newcombe, Rod Laver, Jimmy Conners, as well as the best of the top runners, Bill Rodgers, Alberto Salazar, Patti Catalano, the two Johnny Kelleys, Jim Peters, Gil Dodds, Ron Hill, and on and on.

Always, the running game has been his first love. However, in 1934, long before the name Jock was synonymous with the Boston Marathon, the *Boston Daily Record* picked Jock (then called Johnny) to win that year's race.

"More than half a million men, women, and children will bank the twenty-six-mile stretch between Hopkinton and Boston today to watch 239 runners bid for victory in the 38th Annual BAA Marathon," the paper reported in a story that has changed little in intervening years. "Over the hill and dell, distance runners from all parts of the United States and Canada will vie for the laurel wreath, emblem of victory, and the glory that goes with victory in the Boston Marathon.

"Chief among the veterans, the man for whom half a million voices will send up a thunderous ovation, is Clarence H. DeMar. (Nevertheless) Johnny Semple of the United Shoe Machinery Company, Beverly, Massachusetts, is the *Daily Record's* pick to win the long grind."

Jock did not win. As he said, "I made a mistake and got on the bandwagon and ate a fat steak at Lucky Rock Manor an hour before the race."

Such was the custom in the old days. Runners, seeking to fortify themselves before attempting the twenty-six-mile, 385-yard distance, tried to fit down two-inch steaks in the last moments before dashing to the Boston Marathon starting line.

In Wellesley, Massachusetts he ran strong as the coeds, who formed a narrow corridor, cheered for the runner with the red rosy cheeks. Then cramps hit and he became nauseated from the steak. At Auburndale, just past the seventeen-mile mark where Route 16 turns into Commonwealth Avenue, he walked briefly and lost the pace. He ran again in fits, but his stomach gave in before his legs and will gave out, and he lost his best shot at the one goal that consumed his entire life: to win the Boston Marathon.

"I blew it," he said often from a perch beside a rubdown table in his clinic. "But I achieved my dream. When Johnny Kelley (the Younger) won Boston in 1957, I won standing behind the finish line waiting with a blanket—and my life became complete."

"Jock, the Baron of Glasgow," his friends such as Pat Dengis, Clarence DeMar, and Jimmy Henigan nicknamed him in the 1930s. Jerry Nason, a former *Boston Globe* sports editor, even used the appellation in a column one day.

"Now nobody remembers my real name," said the former Johnny, the Baron of the Boston Marathon, and Glasgow. "They all just call me Jock."

◆

Also called Mr. Boston Marathon, Jock Semple was born in 1903 in Glasgow, Scotland. He brought his carpentry skills to Philadelphia in the years before the stock market crash of 1929, only to discover that the market for carpenters had already crashed. Still, he persevered. To survive, he became a vegetarian and bought broken nuts and old fruit from vendors by the docks.

In 1930 Jock moved to Boston where he took a boy's job for eleven dollars a week. His running helped sustain him through the Depression. Nine times he finished in the top ten at Boston. He ran well enough, and was well enough liked, that Walter Brown, whose father co-founded the Boston Marathon in 1897, set him up with his first physiotherapy clinic in Boston Arena after World War II. Following a massive fire at the arena in the 1950s, Walter Brown, then president of the Boston Garden/Arena Corporation, moved Jock and his clinic to fresher surroundings at Boston Garden.

In later years, the only thing fresh in Jock's Salon were the comments his patients made about Jock's ulterior motives in chasing Kathrine Switzer down the road in the 1967 Boston Marathon. Jock's shove that day boosted women's running more in two seconds than any thousand editorials written in support of women since.

Kathrine Switzer, a Syracuse coed, decided to run Boston when women were still banned from competition, the assumption being in 1967 that distance running could be harmful to women's bodies. Kathrine applied for admission by signing K. V. SWITZER at the bottom of the form. Jock, who screened all entries (often between periods while he worked the Bruins and Celtics games), assumed that "K" was male, and he sent out a number. Even so, Tony Nota, another Garden hand who typed the list of entries, nearly caught the oversight. A week before the marathon, Tony rushed over to Jock's clinic brandishing the application, which was incomplete without a full name. "Jock, you gotta see this," Tony said.

"Oh, blast it, Tony. Don't bother me now. I'm trying to get these men into the whirlpool and the bloody phone hasn't stopped ringing. If I get one more marathon question I'm going to pull the last bloody hairs out of my head."

"Then you don't want me to pull this K.V. joker for not filling out a complete application?"

"Ah, what the heck, Tony. Leave him in now that I've already sent him a number. We're never going to see the imbecile again anyway."

A sportswriter on the press bus was the first to spot "K" the day of the marathon. Two miles into the race, while the press bus wound through the runners, the writer shouted, "Hey, Jock, come look quick. You've got a broad in your race!"

Jock ordered the driver to stop immediately once he discovered this "flagrant violation of the rules." Like a shot he was off the bus, bounding down the road after Kathrine. Though she sped up, Jock caught her quickly, but a wire service photographer on a flatbed truck just in front of the action snapped a picture of Jock in action.

As Jock reached to retrieve his number from Kathrine, her 220-pound boyfriend, who was running beside her, leaned in to plant a broad shoulder indelicately into Jock's ribs. Jock went into orbit and landed in a ditch, but Kathrine landed on *The Tonight Show* (with Johnny Carson) after the photographer's sequence of photos appeared on front pages of newspapers around the world.

Infamy guaranteed! Suddenly Jock became the world's worst ogre. Suddenly, he became public enemy number one of the female gender!

Still, Jock insists he never fell into the ditch.

In 1953 Jock became the co-director of the Boston Marathon, a race that until the mid twentieth century was considered a joke by most Americans. During the 1950s and 1960s, Jock performed nearly all the clerical chores for the marathon. Most people who came through Boston for the marathon dealt with Jock, usually at his Garden clinic. Those who did not meet him in person spoke with him over the device that linked Jock's scathing Scottish brogue indelibly with the Boston Marathon: the telephone.

Will Cloney, Boston Marathon director, described Jock's relationship with the Boston Athletic Association phone, which from the 1950s was located in the Salon: "Tap that phone and you'd have another Jock book," Cloney said. "If you could print it."

Jock's most celebrated telephone explosions came after the sport of running boomed. As he put it, "The infernal device now rings from morning till night. Every time I get my fingers into a patient's sore muscles, another imbecile calls up with some new bloody question."

Invariably, Jock could be prompted to talk running while he was working on a patient. "Running became popular, much to my doctor's benefit, because he was able to stick me for increased heart exams," Jock said. "In the 1970s, the Boston Marathon grew like Topsy, and my headaches grew right along with it. The blasted phone in my clinic never stopped ringing. Some joker would want to know if we were going to have better facilities this year. I'd say, 'Just put your gear in a bag, and into the truck at Hopkinton [the start of the marathon] and you'll get it at the end.' Then he'd want to know about the fac-il-i-ties. I'd say, 'What facilities? You mean hotels, and that?' 'No,' he said. 'Will you have toilets at the start?' I hung up on him. I told him to look for the second tree on the left, or some such tactful remark."

John J. Kelley (the Younger) anchored Jock's Boston Athletic Association marathon team in the 1950s and led the team to a string of national championships. In short, Jock inspired Johnny much as Johnny later inspired Amby Burfoot and Bill Rodgers, who followed them both to the top at Boston.

Johnny Kelley also often offered testament to the mark Jock made on his career—and his life. Here Johnny describes an incident toward the end of his competitive days that added to his appreciation of Jock's words: "Neither shall ye work, neither shall ye eat." Here's the story directly from Johnny.

The Dairy Institute of New York sponsored a fifteen-mile race to finish outside the 1964/1965 New York World's Fair entrance. During the race, my daughter Eileen celebrated her third week in this world, and my friend and Boston Athletic Association teammate Al Confalone lost his job. Still, the big news was that Jock Semple had decided to take a rest.

Nobody at my house in Mystic, Connecticut, could remember a previous lapse in Jock's energy, but Jock told us he preferred to sleep for the night, rather than drive the whole way to New York. After sixteen years of an association (hell, a loving relationship with the Flying Scot), I saw Jock in a light that enabled all the pieces of the puzzle to fall into place. As the man whose hands pounded other people's flesh as incessantly as his feet had for decades pounded pavement quietly climbed the stairs to bed, Al Confalone and I stayed up to chat.

"Jock ragged me all the way down from Boston," Al said, as my wife Jessie joined us. "He never let up on me being out of work. 'Neither shall ye work, neither shall ye eat.' The whole way from Boston, and just me and Jock in the car."

Confalone sought our eyes like a lost puppy. I sympathized with my club mate, the 1959 Pan American Games Marathon fourth place finisher, who now slumped in my kitchen, a beaten fighter. Jock's uncompromising sense of middle-class purpose sure could get to a man at close quarters.

"But Al, you've only been unemployed three weeks," Jessie said.

"That's three weeks more than Jock's code allows," he said. "Now he pictures me hanging out in bars, degenerating."

"That's ridiculous," Jessie offered. "You don't even like the stuff."

"Well, I didn't used to much, Jess, but since Jock's been ragging me up so, I have taken to a little Wakefield Italian bar, just to get my spirits up, mind you."

"Let's pack it in," I said. "Everybody will be more optimistic tomorrow when we head for the race."

My wife took the suggestion. Confalone and I stayed up another half hour to chew the fat, and finish off the quart of Italian port he had begun while waiting for Jock's Toronado to pick him up in Wakefield.

Early fog burned away quickly in the morning. But it wasn't the August sun on my face that popped me awake. Something rustled the foliage outside our open bedroom window, but whatever it was hadn't alerted our dog. I leapt out of bed, pulled on a pair of Bermuda shorts, and headed out. Warm, breezeless sunshine flooded the yard. For an instant, I imagined a world's fair gate shimmering in the asphalt heat waves. Then I was around the house, bounding barefooted toward a figure in the garden.

Jock might have been a fugitive from Millet's painting, *The Angelus*. He stood, shoulders bowed, amid a pile of discarded cherry tomato plants. Laden with succulent, ripe fruit, the plants had prospered as accidentals among my intended crop of F-1 hybrid plants. I had reluctantly uprooted them two days previously. Their lavish crop hadn't spoiled, and if anything, had ripened to their fullest sweetness in discard.

Seeing me, Jock stood straight. "Johnny, did y' know you had a full crop of tomatoes thrown away?"

I assured him I did, that they had been uprooted because they crowded the favored plants. There wasn't any other end for them.

"For cripes sakes, John, they're goin' to waste," said Jock.

"What can I do?"

"Do? Man, get me a bag. Make it one o' them big supermarket bags."

I went into the house and as I pulled a bag from the hallway closet, my wife woke up. "What are you doing, John?"

"I'm getting Jock a grocery bag to fill with cherry tomatoes."

"We don't have any cherry tomatoes."

"Yes we do. Jock found them."

"I thought they were weeds."

"Jock thinks they're food."

"I hope they're not poisonous."

Back in the garden, Jock had made a considerable pile of the juicy red tomatoes. He beamed at the bag.

"Ah, that's the right size. These will last me all week. I'll bring a half dozen to the Garden each day to go wi' my cheese sandwich."

"Jock, Jess worries that you'll eat bad fruit," I said.

"Arrgh! If you knew real hard times like I did, you wouldn't think that at all. Back in the Depression I lived on cherry tomatoes, just like these, for weeks and weeks. I was in Philadelphia, livin' wi' relatives, and I didn't want to burden them wi' extra food bills."

A few minutes later we all set out for the trip to New York, and Jock's huge Oldsmobile Toronado made short work of Connecticut. Conversation between the towns of Mystic and Cos Cob, along the state's southern shore, consisted of Jock's observation about the hard life of the Scottish poet Burns, and his persistence in the face of adversity. "Burns was a farmer," Jock said. "He knew the value of what grew in the ground. He would have known not to throw away those cherry tomatoes. 'Waste not, want not.'"

During the ride a morose Al Confalone sat in the front seat beside the supermarket bag filled with tomatoes. My wife tried to cheer him up while she sat in the back with our two oldest daughters and me.

"Don't worry, you'll find work, soon, Al," she said. "The night is always darkest just before the dawn."

"It's dark in that dive where he hangs out," Jock corrected. "He should be home restin' so he can wake up early to look for honest work."

Confalone shifted under Jock's scorch. Undeterred, the scathing Scot continued, "And, the worst thing of all, he isn't even running. The club needs him, and he has all the time in the world now, and he isn't even running!"

Jock seemed about to explode, but a toll booth forestalled Confalone's complete demolishment.

"All I can say," Jock concluded, as the car regained speed, "is, 'Neither shall y' work, neither shall y' eat.'"

Confalone turned toward my wife. "That's all Jock can say."

In New York, the fifteen-mile race ran true to my expectation for the first ten miles. We baked under a sun borrowed from the

Ancient Mariner's Equatorial calms, and I had to let a young New York Irishman named Norbert Sander amass a huge lead. To run with him would have spelled disaster. I hung on, on the edge of dizziness, in second.

By twelve miles, with the help of Jock's spongings, I began to cut Sander's advantage. But by mile thirteen, I was still more than a quarter mile behind. It would take a miracle for me to win.

The miracle actually transpired. As I approached a bridge that I knew lay only a half mile from the finish, I saw Sander standing still, midway across the bridge. The discovery elated me in a way that only a fanatical competitor who has managed to accept the inevitability of losing can be elated.

Poor Norbert Sander. Stricken en route to a sure win, the New Yorker "let it all go, fore and aft." I sympathized, but with half a mile remaining I pummeled past Sander as he stood posed over the gridding in the bridge.

Several hours later, heading east in the Toronado, we rehashed poor Sander's embarrassment.

"Diarrhea is a problem I had many times in a race," Jock said. "But Sander should have run through it."

"Waste not, want not, eh, Jock?" Confalone quipped.

In that instant I realized the essence of Jock as he shot back: "If a race is important enough to a man, he'll run through anything."

The next week my wife and I got a postcard from Confalone. He had taken a job as a weatherman on the summit of Mount Washington.

"It's a lonely place," he wrote. "But it's a job. And now Jock will talk to me, but I don't have to be there to hear it."

## Chapter Two

"A trainer's got to be cruel to be kind!"
–Jock Semple

To GAIN ACCESS TO Jock's Salon de Rubdown, an athlete would get off the Green Line trolley at North Station and proceed down the steps to Boston Garden. They'd go past the Iron Horse Lounge and make a left onto the stairs that face the "Den for Juvenile Delinquents," as Jock called the electronic pinball parlor in the lobby. Then people walked down a long corridor strewn with candy wrappers and dotted with vendors who sold fresh vegetables, cut flowers, and day-glow Larry Bird posters. Next, they'd turn left to walk up the dark stairs to a door marked BOSTON CELTICS. People continued through the door, but didn't go left toward the Celtic offices. Instead, they turned right, to the steel door with the crooked knob. When they heard whirlpool noises from 6:30 A.M. until the trolleys stopped running they knew they had arrived.

A cartoon hung on the wall in Jock's clinic. It depicts the day of the marathon and the Jock figure, apoplectic, is trying to load the buses outside the Prudential Center and at the same time keep a sharp eye peeled for cheats looking to jump into the race without official numbers.

Jock has his mouth open in the cartoon and his finger is attached to a pot-bellied runner's nose—a suspect marathoner indeed. The man, wearing baggy Bermuda shorts, tries to slip past Jock and get on the bus for a ride to the start at Hopkinton. Nevertheless, he encounters a problem: Jock nabs him.

"Don't tell me you ran 2:18 last month," the cartoon read. "You're a goddamn liar . . . and a bloody fat one too . . . but make sure you pin that number on the front . . . and good luck. Now get the hell on the bus."

◆

"Magic Fingers." That is what hundreds of athletes called Jock's digits. "I don't know if Jock knows the names of all the muscles," John Kelley (the Younger) once said. "But I know his treatments worked for me every time in the 1950s, and made the difference between winning and losing."

Other top athletes concurred. Bobby Orr took a massage from Jock before every hockey game. Soon the rest of the Bruins were making appointments. Bob Cousy took a rub at Jock's clinic whenever he could. So did Russell, and Wilt Chamberlain when he was in town. Walter Brown, the Celtics owner, often joined his players on the table.

Each year Jock set up a table courtside at Longwood in Brookline for the tennis tournaments. "[Jimmy] Conners is my buddy," he once said. "[John] McEnroe I wouldn't give ya two cents for." His method? "I dig in deep with my fingers. A trainer's got to be cruel to be kind."

Johnny Bucyk, a former Boston Bruins captain, insists that Jock added years to his career after he came up with a bad back. Gene Conley, who once played for the Red Sox while serving as back-up center to Bill Russell on the Celtics, claims that Jock could get him into shape faster than any trainer alive. Eventually, to prove that he was no longer a "chauvinist," to demonstrate that he had "reformed," Jock accepted women clients, such as distance runner Patti Catalano. But he always oiled the men first and got them back out on the street before bringing the ladies up.

"My men know the r-r-rules!" he said rolling the R's in his Scottish brogue.

As Jock worked on the day's first batch of clients, he'd tell about the glory days of his BAA marathon team. He'd recount the national championship team, the one Johnny Kelley (the Younger) led. He'd also tell about the time a cop stopped him one cold night near Pittsfield, Massachusetts when he had Johnny and the others in his car. They were all on the way to Detroit for a race.

"The cop said I was weaving and he wanted to take me in for drunk driving," Jock said. "But I told the cop that he should call Boston, that they'd laugh him off the force if he told anybody that he was drunk. Because everybody in Boston knows that Jock Semple never touches the booze."

That led Jock, in a circuitous fashion, to a story about Scotto Gonzales, one of his BAA boys of the 1950s who fell four stories off a building—but still ran a key race for Jock.

"Scotto was one of my good men on the BAA, but I never knew his real name," said Jock. "I never knew if it was Gonzales Scotto, or Scotto Gonzales. He signed it both ways. But even after he fell off a roof he offered to run. He knew we had the Canadian National Championships coming up. He never let a little accident throw him. Scotto was a window washer. He was up in the air holding down a job like the good man he was when the chain around his waist snapped, and . . ." Then, as so often happened in Jock's Salon, the phone rang and the story got put on hold.

"Hello? Who is this? What company? Exterminator company? Yeah, I know about salesmen, the job you have. It's hard times, I know. But I don't want you advertising in the Boston Marathon. That's not our tradition. This is an amateur race, and we don't accept sponsors . . . Look, I said I don't want you driving your car in the race. And I don't want you bringing any signs that say, "They check in but don't check out," or any of your nonsense. But if I do catch you on the course, pal, I have one word of advice for you and your heirs: Keep clear o' me!"

After the call, Jock's current patient on his rubbing table asked, "Who was that, Jock, some guy who beat you in a marathon a hundred years ago?"

"Oh, this is the worst it's ever been. The marathon calls started about two minutes after I came in this morning, I had seven of them, and they haven't stopped yet. Jock reached to pick up the phone again.

"Hello? Yes, this is Jock Semple. But after today if this phone doesn't stop ringing, I'm changing it to 'Simple.' Because that's what your questions are doing to me, interrupting my work. No, I can tell you now, and I know [race director Will] Cloney will second me, we don't need your vacuum cleaner company to help us put on the Boston Marathon. No, it's not in our tradition. We don't take any money, and we don't give any out. No runners get expense money. And they never will. Good-bye.

"Oh, the loonies," Jock said to his patient. "People want to know if the Boston Marathon is going commercial. Over my dead body, I tell them. The runners come to Boston to make their fame. They can go other places to make their fortune. That's our tradition."

"Can you imagine the race ever accepting sponsors, Jock?" the patient asked.

"Sure. But they will have to pay me a nickel for every hour I've given free over the last fifty years. That scares them away. Hello?"

"Easy, Jock," the patient cautioned, "it may be somebody's mother."

"You want to run in the Boston Marathon?" Jock said into the phone. "Have you qualified? You have to have run two hours and fifty minutes in an officially sanctioned race if you're a man. If you're a woman you have to run three minutes and twenty. Which are you? Okay, where the heck is your house? In Germany? Let me know what day you'll be getting in on the plane. I'll have Bill Feeney meet you. He's one of my BAA men. Don't worry, he'll recognize you. Just wear something German."

"Jock, answer me one question," said his patient. "Why would somebody come all the way from Germany to run 26 miles and 385 yards?"

"That's a stupid question."

"Why?"

"Why do you like your wife?"

Jock often told another story from his lifetime in sports. "I've got four patients in my Garden clinic, two lying on rubdown tables and one cooking in the steam bath," said Jock. "One patient is beside the radiator where I keep my grilled cheese warm until lunch. His head is sticking out the little hole at the top and he's reading the *Wall Street Journal*. The fourth man is camped in the whirlpool. I'll move him into the shower in a minute. That way I can advance the others over one place."

Jock went on to say that he had a varied clientele, everyone from bankers to boxers. Two more patients were due in an hour. After that, "Patti Catalano will be back from her ten-mile run," Jock said. "She and her husband, Joe, leave from here at seven in the morning. That's shortly after I get in and before my men come. Patti hurt her hip a couple of years ago. The doctors said she'd never run again. I don't want to go to Massachusetts State Prison for slander, but as far as I'm concerned doctors are 'itis happy.' Bursitis, arthritis. Anyway, they said Patti would never run again. I had Joe bring her up and I started giving her treatments. Now she's the first American woman to go under 2:30 in a marathon."

"Don't you ever get tired?" the patient asked. "Six days a week, ten hours a day. Thirty years you've been rubbing them down. Aren't you ever going to retire?"

"I tried that once. I went to New Hampshire for a week. But I tried to hit the fish with a pole. I'm one guy still in the thick of things, one who has experienced all the transitions in the Boston Marathon, from dirt roads to cobblestones. From concrete to macadam. A lot of years since 1929."

"Any favorites?"

"Yes, two: In 1930 I ran my second Boston Marathon and broke into the big time in road racing. In 1957 young Johnny Kelley (I have to keep telling people that Young John is no relation to Johnny Kelley the Elder, who won in 1935 and 45) broke his bridesmaid role and beat the best in the world to win the Boston Marathon. He set a new American record that day, but more important, he made it respectable for college athletes to run on the roads, which some people, mostly college track coaches, thought were good only for us broken down working guys. Everything that has happened in road racing in America since then, the boom in the sport, can be traced back to Johnny the Younger and his victory in the 1957 Boston Marathon. Let me tell you about that historical importance," he said. But before he could continue the phone rang, again. "Company? What kind of company ya with because I got news for you an' yer heirs . . .?"

## Chapter Three

### "Use the opportunity . . ."
### -Frank Semple to his son Johnny (Jock)

IN 1903, DIXON'S STEEL mill stood on Kidston Street in Glasgow, Scotland, churning out chunks of steel for shipment around the world. Not far from the mill, which locals called "Dixon's Blazes" because the light from the furnace shone night and day, a tightly-packed row of apartment buildings lined the side of the street that abutted the factory wall.

It was on the second floor of one of these apartments that Johnny Semple was born on October 26, 1903, the second son of Frank and Mary Semple.

If fathers back then did a halfway decent job, they tried to prepare their sons to work a trade. When Jock was four, his family moved to Clydebank, a shipbuilding city on the River Clyde. At his father's prompting, Jock went out at six A.M. to take orders from customers who came into the butcher shop down the street. His father said the job would build character. After school, Jock delivered the parcels that the butcher had prepared. For this he was paid a shilling per week. To this meager sum, his father added two cents, which he saved.

Jock's father wanted him to stay in school, but Jock preferred to keep his pockets lined. When he was fourteen he left school to take a job at the Singer Sewing Machine plant where he could work beside his father. Jobs were plentiful, since most factories had adapted to production for the World War I war effort, and Jock was hired immediately.

The downside of his strong work ethic was that young Jock's social life was non-existent. Once in a while he met a girl whose hand he got to hold at a movie, and that sustained him for weeks. Most people had simple pleasures back then.

The street the Semple family lived on was a long row of three-story flats. A newsagent shop bordered one side of the Semple flat, and a haberdashery on the other. Their apartment had two rooms: a main living room and a kitchen, and the family slept in beds in two alcoves. Jock's parents slept in one alcove, and Jock and his two brothers slept in the other. The three boys slept in one bed when they were small, but as they grew older Jock bought a camp bed with his earnings and he opened it each night and packed it up each morning. His mother attended to the chores around the house while the rest of the family worked or went to school. Life was lean in a shipbuilding city.

Shortly after he began to work at the Singer company, Jock was introduced to running. The Singer factory held an annual company sports meet, and Bill Routledge, a professional soccer trainer who lived in the apartment below the Semple's, offered to train Jock along with Routledge's own niece. The niece was Jock's age and turned out to be a pretty good runner. Even then Jock supported women's athletics, but for decades he wore an "anti-woman" label due to the incident with Kathrine Switzer.

Jock won the 100-yard dash at the company meet, and shortly thereafter was recruited by the Clydesdale Harriers, a local running club. At that time, Harrier meets functioned more like interclub social events than tooth and nail competitions. Runners were taught that winning was important, but it was more important to love the idea of running, and to enjoy the exercise fully.

On Saturday runs, the coach split the team into three packs: fast, medium, and slow. Jock ran with the fast pack, which started ten minutes after the other two groups had left. From this style of running, the Americans developed cross country running. Note the parallels. A pace man ran at the head of each group, while a whip trailed at the end. If too much distance opened between the group, the whip blew his whistle to slow down the faster runners. Runners of Jock's time were taught that their basic purpose was to excel as a group, and Jock often said that he owed all the enthusiasm that he brought to club racing to the lessons he learned running with the pack in Clydebank.

Of course Jock was not above organizing a prank or two. Sometimes when he was appointed to take a sack with a shredded paper to mark that day's trail, he'd look for a stream that he knew was deep. He'd lead the trail to the bank's edge, then walk down to a part he knew was shallow and cross there. Once he had splashed across to the other side, he'd recommence dropping paper beside the deep part. Then he'd hide as the pace man led the entire pack face-first into the water. Jock did admit that more than a few times he found himself on the bobbing end after his mates figured out his trick.

Jock improved rapidly as a runner until the day before his six-teenth birthday when he broke his arm in a qualifying race for the Scottish National Championships. Though his arm was placed in a cast, he did not want to reduce his training so he invented a work-out at his job. Jock had many spectators each day as he slipped down to the main gate at the Singer plant to wait for the noon bell.

Each day he tried to get a little extra running in by timing his exit closely with the bell, but one day he missed and his foot touched the ground outside the gate one second before the bell. That afternoon he got a call to go up to the boss's office. The boss was an old fuddy-duddy with a personality like a fish, as Jock described him, and he fired Jock. He also had seen Jock running his weekly soccer score pool, and that may have been a factor, as well.

Jock Semple decided to take his father's advice. Jock knew that if he were to have any security in life he needed to learn a trade, but the economic situation in the country was dismal after the war. It was months before he could find work again. Jock went back to school to learn to become a joiner (a carpenter who uses a fine grade of wood) and sometime during his sixteenth year he found a job as an apprentice house joiner. This skill was to serve him well later, and kept him from starving when he lived in Philadelphia. In Scotland, however, he couldn't support himself on the paltry wages the job paid: the equivalent of three dollars per week, from which he had to buy his own tools. Jock soon left that job, and found work at the John Brown Shipyard where he continued his apprenticeship as a joiner.

John Brown was the main employer in Clydebank. Both the Queen Mary and Queen Elizabeth were built there, but Jock was miserable. When a strike was called, Jock found himself out of work again and became despondent.

"If I were to lend you money for a trip to America, would you go?" his father asked one evening at supper.

This was like a bolt from the blue. "Sure, I'd go," Jock said. His father touched his napkin to his lips. "Use the opportunity," he said. "See what you can do for yourself with a new start, Johnny."

Some years later, during World War II, Clydebank suffered two of the heaviest nights of bombing during the entire war. On successive nights two hundred people died, for a total of four hundred all together. Fortunately, Jock's parents were in the southern part of the United Kingdom at the time. Jock's brother and his wife lived in Wales, in the southwest portion of the United Kingdom, and with news of the bombing possibility his parents had rushed there to be with them. While they were away, the Semple home took a direct hit. Upon return, Jock's father sifted through the rubble, but all he found was a medal Jock had given him after he had won a race in Philadelphia. Jock's father wore that medal for the rest of his life. After his death, Jock's brother sent it to him. Of all the medals Jock ever won, he prized that one the most.

◆

Jock arrived in America by ship, and landed in Philadelphia, Pennsylvania on a bright, sunny day. But, Jock's future was still clouded by uncertainty. During the crossing passengers had been served three meals a day, but Jock joked that with all the sea-sickness he had experienced, he had six meals: three down and three up.

At first, Jock stayed with relatives in West Philadelphia and tried for months to find a job. Finally, he talked himself into a good position as a joiner at the local shipyard. He loved that job.

Then, with summer's arrival, he went into the building trade. One day the boss assigned Jock to work with concrete, a project he attacked with great enthusiasm. Jock needed a brace to hold a wooden trough, but instead of grabbing a scrap piece of lumber, he took a clean board. The boss happened to walk over to watch as Jock cut the piece for the brace far too big.

When he stooped to cut it again, the boss said, "Get your tools."

"What?" Jock asked.

"Pick up your tools," the boss said. "No job is as complicated as you're making it." Bosses held all the cards. Jock was nineteen years old and maturing by the minute.

During this time Jock's social life improved, even if his wallet didn't. Dances were held every Saturday night at the Scottish-American Club in nearby Kensington, and Jock tried not to miss a single one. Sometimes, though, he was forced to skip a dance if a girl got too amorous. Once, he met a girl who began to talk about her future husband. Jock was stunned to think that a girl would go to a dance without her beau, but when he asked where the boy was, she said he was at the dance. That shocked him even more, to think that she would sit on the side of the dance floor and sip a punch with him while her future husband was in the room.

"Where?" Jock asked, as he surveyed the crowd. But she just smiled coyly at him, and his eyes opened wide as he got the message.

"I've got to go to Wilmington in the morning for a carpentry job," he said as he excused himself. He quickly left the dance floor and did not return for two weeks. Jock loved dancing, but there was one thing everyone there knew instinctively: a man who lived on the fringes of unemployment did not flirt with matrimony.

Jock picked up odd jobs and soon was able to move into a ten-dollar-a-week room in West Philadelphia. He joined the Kensington Athletic Club and shortly thereafter became bitten by the marathon bug. When construction began on an exposition that Philadelphia was building for its Sesquicentennial, he found a job laying floors for the Japanese exhibit. The men he worked with talked about the Sesquicentennial marathon, a race expected to draw as many as 150 runners. Jock grew increasingly interested.

Jock decided to enter the marathon and that night he ran ten miles through the streets of Philadelphia. Soon he was running ninety miles a week in preparation, until he dislocated his shoulder at work. Still, he trained with his arm in a sling. He never stopped running.

The morning of the race Jock hitch hiked to the start of the race, which was at Valley Forge. There were only a few marathons in the country then, and the same guys went to all of them. Culver City, California, put on a marathon, but outside of the East Coast the rest of the country remained a desert for road running.

"Do well," a fellow runner said to Jock at the start. Jock later recalled being surprised that anyone even spoke to him.

At the gun he trotted out, but soon moved up with the lead pack, which included a runner named Clarence DeMar. DeMar went on to win seven Boston Marathons and was the bronze medalist at the 1924 Paris Olympics. In this race, Jock fell back as the course wound along the Skuykill River, and then moved inland. The finish was set at a huge stadium in South Philadelphia beside what is today the site of the South Philadelphia Sports Complex.

Jock moved up again, and one of the many spectators who lined the streets shouted, "You're number ten." This heartened Jock, because he knew that only the first ten finishers would get trophies, and he ran like the devil in the hot sun.

The sun beat down fiercely, yet Jock held onto tenth place until he reached the University of Pennsylvania and the twenty-two-mile mark. Suddenly he got a cramp in his leg and was forced to hobble. He soon sensed someone coming up on him, and ran, pulling his leg over the last four miles as he tried to hold off Frank O'Donnell, a Canadian runner who edged ahead of him as they entered the stadium.

Jock kicked, and dragged his leg, but couldn't catch O'Donnell, who beat Jock out of tenth place and a trophy. Jock finished in three hours and collapsed at the line.

Albin Stenroos, the 1924 Olympic marathon champion, had led for most of the race, but Clarence DeMar passed Stenroos to win. Jock lost fifteen pounds during the race and lay gasping on the grass near the finish line. People brought him water, and one man, the man who had said hello at the start, directed the relief efforts.

"You did well," said Bill Kennedy, and he introduced himself as a bricklayer from New York. "Stay with it. But don't be surprised if it takes you at least three years to run a decent marathon."

Jock later learned that Kennedy was dead right. But in this moment, Jock lay still for thirty minutes or more. After he recovered sufficient strength, he took the subway home and was regarded oddly all along the way by the crowd on the train.

◆

In Jock's day, marathon runners were considered second-class citizens. In fact, distance runners were freaks to the general public. Jock remembered a group of runners training along the roads in Philadelphia when suddenly a car swerved in to try to scare them. This was more than a one-time occurrence.

"What're ya runnin' fer, president?" motorists often shouted. Kids pelted them with snowballs, and some runners took to wearing long pants so they could feign being a pedestrian if they crossed paths with anyone.

Yes, distance runners, and marathoners in particular, were considered oddballs, yet they put up with it for the camaraderie and for the joy of running. Jock tried to do everything he could to beat the man next to him in a race. He'd summon every competitive juice, but the minute it was over they shook hands and were friends. But not on the roads. On the roads they gave each other no quarter. That's how life was in the Depression anyway. Most found themselves in and out of jobs, and running served as a way to air out frustration. Runners also carried the main lesson of the road back into their lives: if a man could be tough out there, he wouldn't succumb under normal circumstances.

Most of the runners Jock knew were laborers. Once in a while a college man tried the marathon, invariably without success. Jock and his friends were praised for their sportsmanship and camaraderie, but weren't considered serious athletes. Except in Boston, but then only for one day a year.

Boston has always been the blue ribbon of marathons. Bill Kennedy, who did the most to encourage Jock when he was a young runner, called the prize he won at Boston his "survivor's medal."

In many ways it was. Kennedy, who often took Jock aside at races, was typical of the manual laborers who frequently found themselves unemployed. These men used running to kill the dead time while they waited for a job that rarely came. "Bricklayer Bill," as others called him, was famous for wearing a red, white, and blue kerchief on his head in the Boston Marathon. Kennedy enjoyed his one shining moment in 1917 when he hitchhiked to Boston from New York, and slept on a pool table in a bar in the South End. The next day he won the race, a moment of glory Kennedy spent the rest of his life trying to recapture.

In 1932, Kennedy wrote the following letter to John Halloran at the *Boston Globe*. His feelings were expressed for all runners of that era—and voiced the gap they all felt between being broke on the street and dreaming of winning the gold medal at Boston.


Dear Johnnie:

I am well, but broke. Business is—, but as long as I have my health that is the serious thing. I am looking forward to this year's race. I have been out of work so much this winter that I've had much time to run.

Speaking of Marathon runners, don't you ever wonder what is the lure of it all? What does a Marathon runner think of?

Well, Johnnie, I have run an average of a thousand miles a year for the past twenty-five years. Some do more, some do less, but that average is about 130 hours, along with your mind wandering here and there, building air castles, tragedy and comedy. A runner thinks and pictures so many things.

The lure of the Boston race, Johnnie, is far greater than any in the country and, to me, it is the world. I can only speak of my own thoughts, but I have been close enough to runners for thirty years that I also know their thoughts, hopes, and chances to win the Boston Marathon. That is the dream of every runner. Sometimes I hardly believe I realized that hope fifteen years ago. I am still dreaming, still building castles, and actually believe I am going to win again.

All marathon runners are dreamers. We are not practical. The hours we spend every day, every year! The strength we expend over long, lonesome roads and the pot of gold we aspire to receive for it all! The end of the rainbow, Johnnie, is a survivor's medal.

Boston. To see the name in print, to hear it spoken, sends my blood racing as does the sound of "The Star Spangled Banner." I reached the heights in Boston and also gazed down into the depths. I used to beat my way in these races unnoticed, cold, and half-starved. Then I met Larry Sweeney of the old Boston Globe (Lord have mercy on him) and after that everyone seemed to be my friend.

The 1917 race brings back memory of the ironworker who took me over to the public bath to clean up; the bricklayers who fed me and got me a job; Mr. and Mrs. John Brick, Jack Welsh, Jack and Mrs. Nason and the children who met me at Coolidge Corner with a drink of hot tea; Rudy and Sam Allen, who put me to work; Jack Dailey, who rode a bicycle for me and drank my brandy himself; Al Upham, and his father and mother; George Brown and his boy Walter; yourself; McCabe and the most colorful bunch of newspapermen in the game. You are all strong in my mind when I visit Boston each year. And, I can't forget Edwin Geary of Hornblower and Weeks, whom I have not seen since winning, but his name and face are impressed in my heart.

Chuck Mellor and I didn't have a dollar between us in those days. I had won the Boston race and Chuck finished sixth, but we couldn't eat those trophy cups, nor cash them in and still remain amateurs.

So, the cheapest way to eat was to pay five cents for a glass of beer and fill up on the free lunch that came with it, which some were doing. Then a gentleman, recognizing me from the pictures in the paper, stepped up and asked if I was Bill Kennedy, and was it true about my having two children. When I said yes, he gave me two ten dollar bills, one for each of them. Boy, I could have kissed him; a lucky thing, though, that he didn't me give a third ten for myself, or I would have automatically become a professional.

Well, John, meeting all these people gave me an incentive to show them I appreciated their interest, so I tried hard to win.

Do you know that I always loved the old way best, when they had the bicycle riders with us? It seemed more colorful and made you feel you had a protector at your side.

The people up there in Boston appreciate runners more than anywhere else. No slurs, no wisecracks. Just kind words and applause. Have you ever noticed how sympathetic the young boys are? They are wild at times, but you can't help loving them. Some three or four years ago, the time I finished third, some little kid on a bike, he couldn't have been more than twelve, pulled alongside me at Coolidge Corner. To listen to that boy crooning to me, the words of sympathy his little heart was pouring out, my God, Johnnie, you wouldn't think I was fifty years old to his twelve. Seemed like he was the old warrior and I the child.

Johnnie, I better cut this short. I ran a Marathon in 1924, the hottest day of the year, and I won by over a mile and a half. The officials told me the prize was a beautiful bronze statue of a Marathon runner, six feet in height, too big to carry, and it would be shipped to me by express.

They gave me a receipt (one bronze statue, paid in full). Well, I still have the receipt. But the trophy never came, express or otherwise. Prizes don't mean much to me anyhow. I won the race, which was satisfaction enough for me. I wouldn't give a damn if I fell dead across the line at Boston if I could just win one more time.

The Olympic bait doesn't mean a thing to me. They wouldn't take me when I wanted to go. Hell, I can beat my way to Los Angeles anytime. But I want to beat the Olympic men they do send to the Games. There was never a time, if I had six weeks to train and not work or worry over the wherewithal to run my home and family, I couldn't beat any man on earth.

"Do you know I have seldom come to Boston, or any other race in the last fifteen years, in shape? I dissipated last year before the race, and even the night before, but I ran the course, only to punish myself.

Another attraction in Boston is the old-time runners you meet. Who can but help love Al Monteverde, the biggest dreamer of us all, and probably the wealthiest; little Jimmy Henigan, and DeMar, with his honest but peculiar ways and short answers. A lot of old boys are disappearing, but I try to keep in touch.

Can't you lean back, close your eyes, and picture Tom Longboat and his funny teeth; Festus Madden, over whom I have had many a laugh; Fred Cameron, who became an amateur again in Chicago; great old Sid Hatch, lovable Chuck Mellor, Joe Forshaw, now a millionaire. Mike Ryan and his red head leading the parade in 1912.

Poor Harry Jensen, dying at home in New Jersey, wife and two kids left penniless. Good old Johnny Hayes and a few of the old boys around New York visited Jensen and tried to help. Jimmy Duffy, killed in France; youthful Johnny Miles, Linder, poor Sockalexis, and a host of others who have passed along the long, long trail. They all know "What price glory?" The handshakes, and then oblivion. All we have are the good friends we make.

And that survivor's medal, well, I would rather have a pair of overalls. I can use them if I get a job. But I will be there Tuesday, glad to see the bunch. My feet will be blistered, my legs weary, every muscle aching, but my heart will be happy at the cheers of the crowd. I will be giving them all that's in me too, and I look forward to that little thin string in front of the BAA clubhouse, a cot to lie on, and getting those damn shoes off my feet! So long, old pal, I shall be in the prize winners.

Bricklayer Bill Kennedy

## Chapter Four

"That was the biggest thrill of my life . . . I picked out my
mother's eyes as I kicked the last two hundred yards to the line."
–Jock Semple

JOHNNY KELLEY (THE YOUNGER) said that to his credit, Jock Semple was always accessible to runners during the 1950s. Always. Whether they found him at work in his cubbyhole backroom physiotherapy clinic in the Boston Arena, or after the arena fire at his new cubbyhole in the Boston Garden, Jock never refused a young runner advice. Oh, there were others, men who served as both fathers and confessors for young pavement pounders, but Jock symbolized the era.

A word about the breed. First, they never expected money for their chores. These men, runners themselves during the twenties and thirties, gravitated into advisory roles as this new generation replaced theirs at the front of the pack. Fixtures at the various road races throughout New England, they had suffered the ridicule (and often dangerous hostility) of a generally uncomprehending public.

Theirs was an oral tradition, before the sacred oil could be tapped and bottled like snake oil, before "marathon" formed the essence of cocktail party chatter, before packaged advice to young runners could make the *New York Times* best-seller list for thirty weeks, these men owned the roads. Jock was a man before the running books.

Here's a conversation between Jock and a patient in the steam bath.

"Jock, you've been called the Boston Marathon's staunchest defender. Why are you so staunch?" the patient asked.

"Wouldn't you defend the thing that was like a religion to you?" Jock shot back. "But what bugs me are the number of people who show up the day of the race totally unprepared to run a marathon. They end up jogging with their sixty-two-inch beer bellies. They jog the first mile, then walk two, then jog again. Later it's off to a bar room in Framingham, bend the elbow, catch a cab, and come sprinting down the final straightaway like heroes. They make a mockery of all serious runners.

"But even these comedians aren't the worst. A few years ago, four or five of the leaders were running neck and neck outside Framingham. I was in the press bus when I saw a moron wearing a snorkel and fins pop out of the crowd making snorkel noises. Steam shot out my ears.

"Did the district attorney get you for murder one?" asked the patient.

"No, but I did chase him. This was a couple of years after the incident with Kathrine, and the film crews banged off each other as they got into position on the flatbed truck. It didn't take me long to catch the clown, and I took a dive for his feet, but missed. A policeman followed me onto the bus and said the fellow intended to charge me with assault. The following day the chief of police took the matter into his own hands. 'Look,' he told the snorkel guy. 'If I was Jock, I would have done the same thing. Now get out of my sight before I feed you to Jock.'"

Jock went on to tell about a fellow named Loues, who precipitated all the running in Boston. In 1896 a group of countries got together to work for better relations in the world and recreated the Olympic Games. Loues, a Greek mountaineer, won the first Olympic marathon in Athens in two hours, 55 minutes, and became a national hero in Greece. The Boston Athletic Association paid expenses to take two-thirds of the American Olympic team to the Games that year. While they were there, John Graham, the BAA Secretary, and George V. Brown decided to hold a marathon in Boston, the next year, as a novelty.

"The Boston Marathon was supposed to be run just once," Jock concluded. "Yeah, well, my phone hasn't stopped ringing once."

"So Jock, how did you come by getting the club phone?" asked another patient.

"Call the Boston Athletic Association and you get me. This cinder block palace, boys, that's the BAA in the phone book."

Years ago, Jock explained, the Boston Athletic Association was one of America's most prestigious clubs, on the order of the New York Athletic Club, which has survived and prospered. "The BAA has survived, too. As I say, you're looking at the club's headquarters," said Jock, "but it's only in the past few years that infusion of new blood has sparked a revival."

As a bit of history, at one time the BAA roster included the most proper Bostonians. Founded on March 15, 1887, the BAA once operated a lavish five-story brownstone clubhouse in Copley Square on what is today the site of the Boston Public Library. The clubhouse served for years as the finish line for the Boston, or more exactly, the Boston Athletic Association Marathon. Inside were posh rooms with stuffed wild animals and a giant marlin on the walls.

"Nobody who was member back then lived in a house where laundry hung on a line out the back window," said Jock. "Not like the boarding houses where I lived. These were 'gentlemen,' and the clubhouse reflected their favorite leisure activities: bowling alleys, billiard rooms, five tennis courts, gymnasium, swimming pool, fencing, boxing, big game hunting, bicycle rooms, barber shop, restaurant, parlors, library, and not least, a wine and cigar department.

"The BAA men were the wealthiest businessmen in New England," Jock continued, "but following the 1929 stock market crash, most got wiped out. For me, 1929 was the year I finished twenty-ninth in my first Boston Marathon.

"Think you could help me get finished, Jock?" the patient asked. "I'm dying here in this steam bath."

"You're still carrying some excess weight between your ears. Ten more minutes."

The annual Boston Marathon focused attention on the entire road race season, but only briefly, according to Jock. After the eight-column banner headline in the *Boston Globe* the day of the race, the BAA runners ran in obscurity for the rest of the year.

Boston did not cap the running season. Instead, it kicked it off each year. Throughout the summer runners ran dozens of ten-mile handicap races. Social clubs around New England held picnics in the summer, and always they staged a road race as their festival's featured event. These clubs pulled the best runners in America, because they offered merchandise prizes. It's hard to imagine Bill Rodgers, Frank Shorter, or Greg Meyer running at a picnic today, but in the twenties and thirties, the people who put on these "carnivals" offered wrist watches and toasters, things runners needed to survive. It was the Depression, and often the runners sold or traded the merchandise to get money for food.

Jock's patient was still in the steam bath when he asked. "What happened in 1930?"

"I was twenty-seven years old and that was the start of the Depression," said Jock. "I was out of work and living in Philadelphia, so I hitchhiked to Boston for the marathon. I left Philly on Roosevelt Boulevard at seven in the morning, and I got to Cambridge at nine the next morning."

"Are you going to tell us about the night spots you hit?"

"Night spots!" Jock exclaimed. "If you mean towns up Route 1 such as New Rochelle, Greenwich, Stamford, Branford, Saybrook, and so forth, they were night spots all right. I thought I was going to spend all night in them.

"My last ride," Jock said, "was in a truck. Remember Isinglass curtains? This truck had curtains instead of windows. Oooh, was I frozen. When I finally reached Boston, I took the subway to Scollay Square, then caught the street car to my brother's house in Lynn.

"I was frozen, but hungry to win. Boston was our dream. I ran hard that day, but DeMar won the Boston Marathon for the seventh time. At Natick, the ten-mile mark, I was running in fifteenth place. By the Newton Hills, I began to move up. I had been told that the first eight finishers would win medals, and I wanted one so badly. I moved into the top ten at Coolidge Corner, past Johnny Miles, who had won the race twice before, and Dave Fagerlund, one of the top Finns. I passed Bill Kennedy, who had become my good friend and mentor, passed Silas McLellan of Nova Scotia, and Gordon Norman of Malden. Then I moved onto Jimmy Henigan's shoulder. Willie Kyronen and Karl Koski, both great Finnish American runners, battled to catch DeMar. I hung onto Henigan, who would become an American Olympian two years later, and with two miles to go I passed him. I kicked hard to finish seventh, ten minutes behind DeMar's 2:34:48. That was the greatest day in my life, but the Philadelphia papers bollixed it up.

"WEST PHILADELPHIA IRISHMAN HITCHHIKES TO BOSTON AND FINISHES SEVENTH," read the headline in the Philly paper the next morning.

"What's wrong with that?" Jock's patient asked. "They gave you ink."

"I'm no Irishman," said Jock. "Still, that was the biggest thrill of my life, because my mother was visiting my brother and she attended the race. I picked out my mother's eyes as I kicked the last two hundred yards to the line. She was standing in front of the BAA clubhouse clapping and I swear I had tears in my eyes.

"I got fired two days later though, after I hitched back to Philadelphia. I don't go for excuses, but in this case the boss was laying for me because I was a runner. I had taken time off from my job to hitch to Boston and employers generally had nothing but scorn for marathon runners. They were more impressed with the elbow-benders, the guys who came to the job hung over but with stories to tell. 'Oh, Joe, I saw you Friday night. You and that floozy at the saloon!' That kind of thing.

"I had a good job, and I was sorry to lose it," said Jock. "The streetcars in Philadelphia were brought in regularly for inspection, and my crew took the old seats out and replaced them with new ones. My feet hurt after Boston, so at one point I changed my shoes. I put on a pair with rubber soles, but the boss called me over. 'What do you got on your feet?' he said. 'Those aren't the shoes you wore to the job this morning. Get your tools, kid. I don't need anybody on my crew who takes a break before the bell.'"

After that he went home, Jock said. He packed up his things, and moved to Boston. From then on he was a confirmed New Englander. He'd been offered opportunities to open clinics in different parts of the country over the years, but he'd always refused. One man wanted to give him a health spa in California with Greek statues without clothes, as he put it, but Jock said no, not for any sense of modesty—simply because he never wanted to leave Boston.

"Also, I was afraid if I accepted any of the offers I might be forced to be polite to everybody, even phonies, and that's a skill I never acquired," said Jock. "The Lynn YMCA gave me a job as a locker room attendant when I first arrived in town in 1930. Previously the job had been done by high school boys, but the Depression had hit with full force by then and I felt lucky to have any work. The job paid eleven dollars a week, barely enough to live on, but the worst part was my having to accept charity from my brother.

"The eleven dollars paid for fruits and nuts," he continued, "which I bought from vendors at open air markets, but I had scant money left over to give my brother James for rent. I slept on a daybed in the living room and bought him a ton of coal whenever I could. I did give him some my prizes, including a gold watch I won at a road race."

During this time Jock took two long training runs a day, mostly because he had the time. He was punching the bag in the gym one day when Earl Mills, the YMCA coach, suggested half-jokingly that he start a team. But a light bulb flashed above his head and Jock began to recruit some of the athletes as he stood in the cage at the Y. As they paid their three cents for a towel, Jock made his pitch. Soon he had a good crop of potential star runners.

"Mills became the coach, and I captained the team," Jock said. "With runners such as Tom Bury, who was to become a regular top-ten finisher at Boston, Frank and Larry Reed, Tony Paskell, and Andre Brunnelle, we won team championships up and down the East Coast, including the national championship in Baltimore in 1931."

To keep the team on the road, Jock made speaking appearances at the Kiwanis and Rotary Clubs in the Lynn and Revere area. After a rousing speech, local small businessmen passed the hat and helped collect twenty- or twenty-five dollars for gas. That was all Jock's team needed, as they brought our own food. Gas was eight gallons for a dollar and twenty-five dollars covered expenses for six of them.

"It was on one of those trips that I met Fred Brown," said Jock with a smile. "Since the 1930s, Fred and I have been confirmed friendly antagonists. One weekend a local car dealer lent us a seven-passenger Buick to take down to York, Pennsylvania for a road race. Since we had an extra seat I invited Fred, a milkman from Medford and the captain of the North Medford Club. Fred tells the story, which is a complete lie, that I brought a jar of goat's milk with me for strength and the jar went sour, forcing abandonment of the car in New Jersey.

"Fred did great work keeping the spirit of road racing alive in New England the past forty years as a handicapper and chairman of the long distance committee. Oh, he was a pain though, and dictatorial too. Fred could get me madder than a bee in a jar, but he's done a lot of good for the running game.

"York, Pennsylvania. Know the product for which it is famous?" Jock asked. "We won the team championship on that trip, after which the mayor of York invited us up to the speaker's platform to accept our merchandise prizes: Bar-bells! The mayor and other local dignitaries presented the first place finisher with a five-hundred-pound bell, the second man received 250, and so on, until we all had to cough up a week's pay just to pay for the gas to lug those prize items back to Boston.

Jock did well in races during that time. He won the Novelty Park Marathon in Pawtucket, Rhode Island in 1931. It was a rainy day and the roads were muddy, but he went out with the leaders and by the mid-point in Woonsocket, only Les Pawson was with him. They battled together for about three miles before Jock managed to pull ahead and win in 2:44:32.

Pawson was the speed man of Jock's era, the first one among that group to appreciate the benefits of training on a track. When Pawson, who had been born in England, set the record at Boston with a 2:31:10 clocking in 1933, he ran the last six miles into a biting wind. After he finished, his arms were lobster-red on the front and white on the back. Jerry Nason estimates that the wind took six minutes away from him. Still, Pawson was a humble guy. He never said, "I could have done 2:15 today." Instead, he remarked in a post race interview, "Someday somebody is going to run 2:25 on this course." Jock gave a lot of credit to Pawson, because he knew the value of speed.

Beginning in the 1930s and extending into the 1940s, four men dominated the Boston Marathon: Pawson (a winner three times, in 1933, 1938, and 1941), Johnny Kelley the Elder (the 1935 and 1945 winner), Pat Dengis (who finished on the heels of the winner a number of times), and Ellison "Tarzan" Brown (the winner in 1936 and 1939).

Clarence DeMar won for the seventh and last time in 1930. The new generation, led by Johnny Kelley the Elder, Pawson, Dengis, and Tarzan, together with Gerard Cote, a Canadian, defined marathon running in North America before John Kelley the Younger opened the doors for the college men who continue to dominate today.

Tarzan was certainly the most colorful. Today, we can only speculate how great he might have been had he been trained properly—trained at all, for that matter. But it was Jock's guess that Tarzan, a Narragansett Indian from near Westerly, Rhode Island, could have been the best 10,000-meter man in American history. Jerry Nason shared Jock's opinion, as he once wrote:

> The trim brown shanks of Ellison Myers Brown have caused many a professional coach to grind his teeth in exasperation. Throughout the 1930s those streamlined legs sent the Indian pelting over the roads, when really they were meant to win Olympic track titles and races from the Finns.
>
> Tarzan Brown had the misfortune to be born poor, and in rustic surroundings. As a boy he guddled (a Scottish word meaning grasping fish by the hands) for trout with his bare hands. He roamed the woods. He was more at home in a tree than out of it; hence the name, Tarzan.
>
> His schooling was sketchy. Tarzan would much rather learn to keep a good line of traps than to explore the alphabet. He could run all day through the woods and brush without tiring.

"I have my own Tarzan story," Jock said as a follow up to Nason. "A trainer named Tippy Salimeno had been training another Indian runner in Rhode Island, a fine prospect named Chief Stanton, when Salimeno first met Tarzan. Stanton was out on the roads doing fifteen miles, when an eleven-year-old kid appeared from behind a bush and ran silently on Chief's heels. For more than three-quarters of the workout the boy shadowed Chief without saying a word, just puffed along behind him. Finally, in the last two miles, Stanton pulled away, and as he arrived at the appointed spot where Tippy sat waiting for him in a car, Salimeno shouted, 'Great time. Very fast, come on through.'

"Stanton was too tuckered out to speak. Instead, he pointed behind him. As he finished he said, 'You think I ran fast. Tippy, there's a boy about ten years old right behind me.'

"The two waited, but no boy showed. To prove to Tippy that he wasn't crazy, Chief led Salimeno on a hunt for the boy, and finally they found Tarzan, who had ducked back into the bushes, sitting under a tree. Salimeno befriended him and later became his trainer too.

"Years later, after Tarzan had won the Boston Marathon he said, 'Trainer Salimeno deserves great credit. He kept encouraging me. He kept my pep up.'"

It wasn't for lack of trying that Salimeno couldn't instill more self-discipline in Tarzan. It's just the way Tarzan was. He died in 1975 when he was struck by a van in a parking lot outside a bar. Stories circulated that he had argued with the driver inside the bar and they carried the fight outside to the parking lot, but Tarzan's friends and family disputed this. At any rate, Tarzan was a free spirit.

Jerry Nason, writing in the *Boston Globe* in 1943, had an interesting comment.

Tarzan's natural ability was so great that even midway in his career as a road runner, when his sweeping stride was broken down to a macadam gait, they put him on a cinder track and raced him against the watch just to see what would happen. He ran the mile in 4:28, fast enough to beat almost any college miler in New England.

The Indian would give a dietician the heebie jeebies. He eats and drinks anything that appeals to him. Training is a haphazard affair for him at best. At various times he has been a stone mason, a farmer, a wood chopper, a laborer, a stevedore, and is presently working in a defense plant at Westerly.

While he was doing a hitch as a stevedore, a steel door fell on him and inflicted a five-inch gash across his thigh. Tarzan quickly applied a tourniquet, but all he said was, "Hope this doesn't stop my running."

When he was at Berlin in the 1936 Olympics, just about all the Americans thought the Indian would make hash of the Japanese and the rest in the big marathon race. Tarzan had a fondness for German beer, however, and on top of that he got into trouble. He picked on a couple of Nazi black shirts and rapped together a couple of their heads.

Also, he suffered from a hernia, which he never mentioned, even after that still he looked like an Olympic winner at sixteen miles, then dropped out, wrote Nason.

"Tarzan only made the Olympic race after the Americans sprung him from jail following his fight with the Nazis," Jock said of Tarzan Brown. "Asked why he got into a fight with them, he told me, 'I didn't like them,' meaning the Brown Shirts. 'I remember the day he left with the Olympic team in 1936. He went down to the boat and began climbing up on the smokestack. I asked him why he did that. He said he wanted to see Germany. He didn't believe the boat could go there unless he could see the other side of the ocean first.

"John Kelley the Elder, who ran his first Boston Marathon in 1928, ran in the Berlin Olympics. In 1981 John the Elder completed his fiftieth Boston. John the Elder and I have been close since

my earliest days in Boston. We used to squeeze into cars and ride
to races throughout New England. We'd stay over in dollar-a-night
hotels in our younger days, just to run."

John the Elder was born in West Medford, Massachusetts in
1907. The oldest of ten children, he attended Arlington High.
When he was thirteen years old, his father took him to the Boston
Marathon and he saw Frank Zuna win.

"That day he decided that he would be a marathon runner,
which is how true it is that one generation inspires the next," said
Jock. "No man in the history of the event has lost more Boston
Marathons in the last three miles than John Kelley the Elder. Twice
he won, and seven times he finished second. Nineteen times he
placed in the top ten. Had he not been so frail, John the Elder
might have turned some of those second place finishes into victories. Still, like us all, he knew that running paid nothing, and nothing beat the satisfaction of landing a job. If the fame that came
from winning a Boston Marathon helped, well, then so much the
better."

"These handshakes and the glory that goes with this
marathon business are okay," John the Elder said after he finished
second to Walter Young in 1937. "But a job would be lots better.
I've been unemployed for the past two months, and trying to look
for a job and train for the big race was just too much of a burden,
I guess. I know one thing: I could run a lot better if I had the peace
of mind of a fellow with a job."

Finally, Boston Edison hired him, and that company had the
wisdom to build a track club around him.

"After I beat Les Pawson at the Novelty Park race in 1931, a
group of well-wishers grabbed me and whisked me into a training
room for a massage, part of the special treatment accorded the
winner," said Jock. "They put stuff on me, it must have been horse

liniment, and that was the worst torture! They put their fire all over me, even in the most delicate places, and I hopped off the table finally and ran into the showers. But even that didn't cool off the delicate places. I was red hot, and all I could do to ease the pain that night was go to a YMCA dance in Lynn.

"There I was honored as the New England champion, but I kept on moving. It didn't hurt so much if I flailed my arms and legs. The girls loved it. Nobody put more into dancing than I. Though I got home at midnight, I couldn't sleep and I walked the streets of Lynn waiting for 5:01 A.M. and the first newspaper delivery truck to arrive. Suddenly one appeared and I bought a dozen papers right off his truck. It was five in the morning, the sky was black except for a red strip behind the stores on the east side of the street. I fumbled through the top paper, while I held a dozen more between my knees, and I saw it: my name in headlines for the first time in my life. I only wish Tim Horgan could have been writing then, when I was genuinely famous—before "infamous" became a prefix for Jock Semple.

Behind Jock, the patient in the hot box held up a white towel as a white flag. "Jock you said only ten more minutes!"

## Chapter Five

"Fear the man who comes to the race with his clothes in a paper bag. That's your real runner."
–a favorite adage from the 1930s running era.

TODAY A MODERN RUNNER'S ENTIRE assortment of equipment weighs less than one of Jock's old shoes. He ran Boston Marathons over dirt roads when the chiropodist's station at the finish line in front of the Lenox Hotel looked like a butcher shop.

The runners all had their own preferences for toughening their feet. Jock once met a man who had participated in Bernard McFadden's much-hyped six-day runs. He used fish brine. Pickle brine also worked, as did sea salt water, but fish, though it smelled to high heaven, toughened feet the best without hardening them. Jock adopted the fish approach and was continually astounded at the compassion displayed by his fellow boarders in the ten-dollar a week rooming houses where he lived. Three nights a week, every week, he placed a pan of fish brine under the desk in his room while he sat down to write letters home and toughen his feet. Either the Irishman, Poles, and Italians who bordered his room wore clothespins over their noses, as Jock was tempted to do, or they were fans.

Sam Ritchings, a local shoemaker approached Jock in the early 1930s to ask if he'd participate in an important experiment. Jock was lying on a cot at the finish of the Boston Marathon when Ritchings said he had an idea to reduce friction and prevent blisters. Jock told him if Ritchings could do that, he'd be everyone's hero. Bob Campbell, the former National AAU long-distance chairman, often told the story of a guy who put a dollar bill in his shoes before the Boston Marathon. When the guy took his shoes off at the end, the bill had been torn into ten pieces. If Sam could save runners that pain, Jock told the old shoemaker he'd gladly volunteer.

Over the next few months, Jock tested shoes Ritchings made for him, but they always fell apart. Never one to quit, Ritchings, who wore a black cape and labored at night with his hands, redesigned the shoe and produced another pair. This time he used white buckskin. The white surface reflected the heat, whereas the standard black shoes the runners all wore absorbed the heat. Ritchings did a computation and estimated that the white shoes radiated 38 percent less heat than the black shoes. In addition, the white buckskin was more durable. He put elastic into the innersole to allow freer movement for the foot, and he left out the stiff heel counter to prevent abrasion. The sole was crepe and had a metacarpal pad. Importantly, he added perforation to the sides of the shoes, which allowed ventilation.

The shoes were a dream and soon Jock was the envy of all the other guys who lay on cots with bleeding feet. As Jock sauntered by in white dogs, many let out a howl. But soon everyone wanted a pair, and within weeks Ritchings was swamped with orders. John Kelley the Elder and DeMar received Ritching's second and third pair. By the mid-1930s, every top marathon runner in America was wearing the S.T.A.R. Streamlines. Ritchings used his own initials:

Sam T. A. Ritchings. To this he added Streamline, because that's
what the shoes were, sleek, the white bucks of the roads.

Interestingly enough, Ritchings did not apply for a patent
until a full year after he introduced his shoe. He was in no hurry,
he said. It took him sixteen hours to make one pair, for which he
charged $7.50, but money did not matter to him. "Somebody may
make a shoe that looks like mine," he said. "But nobody could ever
duplicate my S.T.A.R. Streamlines because there's too much of me
in my work." When Ritchings died in 1937 at age seventy all the
runners felt a great loss.

◆

1932 proved to be Jock's Olympic year that never was. He did not
run Boston in 1931. Smilin' Jimmy Henigan won, which was fitting
since Jimmy, like John Kelley the Elder after him, was a crowd favorite. The "Smilin'" was a misnomer, however. Jimmy only looked
as if he was smiling when he ran. Actually, he once said, "That's
not a smile, that's agony they see on my face."

"Fear the man with the paper bag." That was Jimmy Henigan's favorite expression, according to Jock. He was never impressed by the dandies who came to Hopkinton in department
store sweat suits. Instead, "Fear the man who comes to the race
with his clothes in a paper bag. That's your real runner."

Jock came in tenth in the Boston Marathon in 1932, and
knocked a minute off his 1930 time. A month later he won the
Pawtucket Marathon and beat DeMar's record with a 2:39:25. He
was keyed now for the Olympic Trials, scheduled for June in Washington, DC, but almost instantly frustration overwhelmed him. It
wouldn't have bothered Jock so much to be left off the team, but
he was clearly running well enough to make the Olympic team.

Jock Semple filed a second time for US citizenship, a process he had first initiated in 1923. But, he was told that the year he spent in Scotland in 1928 made his first application void. He now would have to reapply all over and wait five additional years before he could file again.

No way. Jock got affidavits to prove that he had stayed in Scotland for a year because his mother was sick, which she was, but after much aggravation, a clerk showed him the small printing on the form that said, "After seven years void for ALL reasons."

That shot Jock's chances for the US Olympic team; but there was always the Union Jack—or so he thought.

As he told his patients many times in his clinic, Jock wrote to England and learned that the British were taking two marathon runners instead of three to the Los Angeles Games: Duncan Wright, and the veteran Sam Ferris. Jock became very excited at this news. Running on an Olympic team had become the other half of his life's goal, and Jock believed he would be picked after this strong run in the 1932 Boston Marathon. Since Boston (from London), was halfway to California anyway, Jock wrote to the British team officials to tell them that his inclusion on the team wouldn't cost them a dime. Jock offered to pay his own way, which meant he intended to hitch.

No thank you, they said.

Hoping to improve his chances, Jock hitched to Toronto for the Canadian qualifying marathon. He got a little training in on this venture and even spent a night in jail. You see, Jock never stood on the side of the road when hitch hiking, he explained. Instead, he jogged. It kept him in shape and took him closer to his destination. Jock never bought food in restaurants either, as he had no money for anything except grapes and apples, which he kept in his pocket. Often the drivers who picked him up told stories about their running prowess as boys, and Jock said he met more ten-second, 100-yard dash men in those days than the Boston Marathon has runners today. Jock quickly learned to nod his head whenever the stories began, which invariably earned him a couple of extra miles in the car.

One night, Jock got put in the cooler in upstate New York, but he was quite willing to cooperate. It was late in the day when he was left off in a small town in Cherry Valley, New York. He told a policeman who stopped him that he was a runner going to Canada to run a marathon. They had a drunk in the tank already, the policeman said, but he offered Jock the cell next to the drunk's if he wanted a cot to sleep on.

"Sure," Jock said, and he slept right through the night, even with the guy next to him banging on the bars with a tin cup. In the morning the police offered to give Jock a meal ticket to the local Y for breakfast, but Jock refused, not wanting to accept charity. He figured the police had been kind enough to him, and besides, he still had some grapes in his pocket.

Jock made Toronto in two days at the cost of five cents, which would have made his frugal ancestors proud. His only cost was when he walked across the bridge from Niagara Falls into Canada and paid the nickel toll.

In Toronto Jock got in touch with Ernie Wyer, the brother of Canada's great runner, Percy Wyer. Ernie put him up in the Y where he got a shower and a good night's sleep before the marathon.

"How do you like this?" Ernie asked, as he showed Jock the race trophy before he bunked down.

"Gee, Ernie," Jock said. "It's nice, but when I win a trophy I like it to have a lid on it." A lid is a statue of a runner at the top of a trophy. This trophy did not have a statue on top.

"Get a lid on this trophy," Ernie said as he turned to one of the officials. Then he turned back to Jock. "That should offer added incentive for you in the race, Johnny."

It did, but Jock didn't win the trophy. He was leading the pack when he got hit with the runs at eighteen miles. He dashed into the woods and put himself back in as quickly as possible, and was still in the lead until Eddie Cudworth overtook him in the last three miles and nipped him for a spot on the Canadian Olympic team.

Later, Jock wrote more letters to British team officials, but his pleas did no good. He proved he had beaten Eddie Cudworth earlier, had defeated Paul DeBruyn (the German Olympian and a Boston Marathon winner), beaten both Jimmy Henigan and Hans Oldag of the United States, and defeated more than a dozen of the world's best. But even though he offered to pay his own way to Los Angeles, those old fogeys, as he called them, would not relent.

◆

During this time one of the most significant developments in marathon history was occurring. Barely any mention of it was made in the Boston papers, except for a little box that appeared on the sports page, but Paavo Nurmi, the Finnish Olympian, ran a qualifying marathon for the Olympics—his first attempt at the distance—and not only made the Finnish team, but shattered the world record by ten minutes. In 1932, when Pawson held the Boston record with a 2:31 clocking, Nurmi ran 2:21. That his feat received scant notice in the Boston papers indicated the low regard paid to marathon runners in America.

Actually, if you can imagine a totem pole that represented the hierarchy of sports, marathoners were the part that goes in the ground, as Jock expressed it.

Later, however, Paavo Nurmi was suspended from the Finnish team for a spat that involved expense money. He believed he was being short-changed, and after he refused to compete in any additional German Federation meets, he was barred from competing in the Olympics.

This wasn't bad news for an enterprising group of Boston promoters, however; they saw opportunity, as Jock explained it to patients in his clinic. They sought to capitalize on the Nurmi fiasco. When the suspension held and Nurmi was forced to sit the Olympics out, the Boston Olympic Club conjured a promotion for Rockingham Park, a little-used Thoroughbred race track in Salem, New Hampshire. The promoters announced that Nurmi (whose suspension they believed would soon be lifted) had agreed to compete in a "new" Olympic marathon at Rockingham Park. Then Juan Zabala of Argentina, who had just won the 1932 Olympic marathon, signed on to accept Nurmi's challenge to run face to face. This delighted Jock, of course, as he wanted a crack at Zabala after missing the Olympics himself, and for six weeks he doubled his training.

Nurmi came, but his suspension was not lifted so he could not run. Instead, he could only serve as the race's starter. Before the race began, however, Zabala announced that he was going to attempt to break Nurmi's world record, which stoked great interest.

The runners lined up, and bang! Nurmi fired the gun and the runners were off. Zabala looked as if he might fulfill his promise, as he jumped out front early. John Kelley the Elder went with him. Kel was just a boy then, and had not yet proven himself as a great marathon runner. Nevertheless, he put himself in Zabala's back pocket. Jock was in fifth, and as he watched Kel he thought he was playing the rabbit for his pal Henigan. Years later, John the Elder told Jock he had misjudged the quickness of Zabala's pace, and truly thought he could keep up with the Argentine. In retrospect, John was great as a ten-miler, which might explain his reasoning.

Zabala and Kel ran away from Jock and the rest of the runners, who formed a pack: DeMar, Henigan, Whitey Michaelson, New York's top runner of that period, Bricklayer Bill Kennedy, Clyde Martak (who earlier had won the national championship at Washington, DC), and Jock. After a few miles Jock turned to Kennedy and said, "If Zabala holds this pace, I'll race you for second." Kennedy shot him a knowing look.

After twelve miles, however, Zabala stepped off the track. He said he had new shoes that pinched his feet, but Jock never went for excuses, he told his patients. The man simply went out too fast and crapped out.

The rest of the pack settled down and Jock soon passed Kel, who had begun to crack under the hot sun. At that point Jock took the lead, which he held for eight miles. Later, he didn't know if he was crazy, or merely over-excited about the company, but he stretched his lead to a half-mile at the eighteen-mile mark. Then it hit him again: the runs. He scooted into the woods as the crowd in the grandstand stood and stared, confused. He worked quickly, and when he came back out running he still had a lead, but he had been weakened and ran stooped over as the crowd applauded, now that he was running again.

At twenty-two miles Whitey Michaelson caught Jock. Whitey was strong and he kicked, and he licked Jock by about half a mile. Jock took second, while DeMar finished third. The first place trophy was an enormous thing, and Jock had to suppress envy as he watched Whitey Michaelson accept it. Jock got a pretty nice cup, but the difference was like caviar and canapés. He got a big hand from the crowd, but the next day he was back in the cage at his eleven dollar a week job: a club hero, but still broke.

Jock piled on the marathons. A few weeks later he successfully defended his New England marathon title by winning the Manchester race, but the next day he got a letter from Bill Kennedy asking if he'd hitch to New York, for the Portchester Marathon. Jock looked at the date. The race was two days away. His legs were still sore from Rockingham and Manchester, yet he had to go for Bill's sake. Bill was the founder of the Portchester Marathon and he needed top-flight runners. He was having trouble getting sponsors without big names, and though it meant running two marathons in four days, Jock went because it was important to Bill.

When Jock arrived, he was shocked. Bill had come up with the idea of a "handicap" marathon to attract newspaper attention, and he had put Jock on scratch. Not only were Jock's blistered feet killing him, but he had to wait forty-five minutes while the other runners were sent off ahead. Jock had never been so restless. Pat Dengis was allotted fifteen minutes, but in a fine gesture offered on behalf of Jock's sore dogs, he forfeited half of it.

Bill Steiner (an Olympic runner from New York) and Jock formed the last of three groups to go off. Jock was so stiff he felt as if he was running on stilts. But, by the ten-mile mark Jock began to unwind, and by twenty miles he had caught the entire field, except for Pat Dengis. Soon Jock pulled even with Dengis, but then he died. Only encouragement from friends along the course kept him moving. Jock took sixth, but finished with the second fastest time. He was happy with the two silver medals he received, one for second in the handicap category and the other for total elapsed time, but nothing beat the appreciative look in Bill Kennedy's eyes as he took Jock aside and said, "Thanks!"

Shortly thereafter, Jock was fired. Even at eleven dollars a week he was too expensive, and the Y fired him so they could give club members a chance to work off their dues behind the locker room cage. With nothing better to do Jock hit the road. But a fortunate thing happened and Jock received some very wise counsel that was to guide him toward a life long career in sports.

Unemployed and desperate, Jock decided to join C.C. Pyle's commercial cross-country runs. "Cash 'n Carry" the runners called Pyle, as the man was widely regarded to be a fly-by-night operator. Cash 'n Carry operated a running circuit up and down the East Coast, which many say he rigged. By the time his troupe pulled into a town, Cash 'n Carry had already stationed himself in front of the local saloon and was taking bets. "Miraculously" the runner who lived closest to that town won the day's prize for fastest elapsed time between the town the run started in and the town the run finished in—except, of course, when the odds made it more practical to "tilt" the race to the man from East Oshkosh, or Timbuktu, or whatever cow-town fit that. Still, it was a job and Jock was on his way to sign up when he stopped at Al Monteverdi's home, a veteran of one hundred-plus marathons and friend to many of the young runners. When Monte heard of the plans, he blew up.

As some relevant backstory, the Amateur Athletic Union had been formed in 1888 for the express purpose of curbing unscrupulous promoters such as C.C. Before then, athletics beyond college competition came under the control of those who exploited them for profit. It was not uncommon before 1888 to find promoters who announced prizes of substantial worth to attract both athletes and huge crowds. Upon collection of gate receipts, however, winners of the race might discover that the promoter had departed with the prizes.

All this is documented in the 1937 book *The Encyclopedia of Sports* by Frank Menke. Other promoters, those who advertised a "strictly amateur" meet, might give a trophy to the winner in full view of the audience, after which the promoter and the victorious athlete met in a remote or sheltered spot. The winner gave back the trophy, got cash, and the promoter started shining up the trophy to award to some other "amateur" at a later promotion.

It was not hard to see how "Cash 'n Carry" became a nickname.

Since these meets offered the only outlet for both noncollege and post-college men to compete, the AAU, which was regrouped as the Athletics Congress, was created to remove non-professional sports from all taint of exploitation. In other words, their goal was to make running "pure," to place it beyond the clutches of the abusers.

"Don't throw your amateur status away on a crook," Monteverde wisely said to Jock.

Monty, as runners called him, held the official record for walking across the United States: seventy-nine days, ten hours, and ten minutes from New York to San Francisco. He was sixty-nine years old when he accomplished the feat. In the course of his walk, he wore out the two twenty-five-year-old aides he had hired to drive beside him.

"I'm broke, Monte," Jock said, as he toweled off after a hard workout on the track Monte had built behind his house. Monte, a veteran of 110 marathons, fixed Jock with steel gray eyes.

"Running will be good to you in time," he said, as he walked back to the house. Then he added, "Don't be a damn dope and blow it."

Before long, Monte became a prophet. Jock went back to Boston, and was in the offices of the United States Shoe Machinery Company applying for a job when one of the younger company officers recognized him. "Jock," he said, "you're just the man."

"I am," Jock replied, more as a statement than a question. "Whaddya need?"

"We've got a bit of a problem," the young man said. "I need to establish a road race. The general manager has entrusted me with responsibility for putting on an event at the carnival that United Shoe is going to hold on the lawn this spring."

The fella was smiling, and Jock could see that he wanted the information for free.

"I'm here applying for a job," Jock said, and the young man's smile disappeared. "What I'm saying is, I'd love to help you out."

The younger man finally made the connection because he said, "Oh, I see," and he took Jock's application from a fat pile his secretary had amassed and walked into a paneled room. A moment later he signaled for Jock to follow him.

During the meeting, the employment manager was called in, and Jock pitched his idea to a group of four executives: "I can form a running club for you," Jock said. "I'll bring the national championship to United Shoe, just as I did for the Y in Lynn. But I want a job." He mentioned that he was a carpenter, but the employment manager shook his head.

"We're all filled up with carpenters," he said. "Can't expect an opening for a year. Maybe eighteen months."

"Then I'll sweep the floor," Jock said. "I'm hungry. I'll do anything."

"You're hired," the four said, nearly in unison.

Jock was assigned to the die department where he learned how to sharpen cutting dies that were used to stamp out leather for making shoes. His bosses estimated that it would take him six months before he became proficient enough to go on piece work. In the meantime, Jock made the fantastic beginners rate of forty cents an hour for a forty-hour week. He took home sixteen dollars each week, and soon was able to pick up four extra hours on Saturday mornings washing the floor in the shop. It was better than pick and shovel work in zero-degree weather, which is what he had been doing since the Y had laid him off.

Jock contacted several of his ex-YMCA runners and enlisted others in the factory who had run for Beverly High School. Before long he had assembled a fine team, and they made their debut at the North Medford twenty-miler in March, 1935. Maybe it was the steady job. Or, maybe it was the new accommodations he was able to afford in a boarding house, or the load he felt lifted from his shoulders after he no longer had to sleep on his brother's daybed, but he found himself at the front of the pack. The race came down to a three-way contest between John Kelley the Elder, Dengis, and Jock. By seventeen miles, Kel pulled away—wearing a pair of S.T.A.R. Streamlines—but Jock's team won the team championship. That propelled them toward Boston, which they also won for their team, and finally toward the nationals in Washington, DC.

There, the United Shoe team defeated fourteen of the top teams in the world, including the Finnish-American and German-American clubs, which boasted two greats, Mel Porter and Paul DeBruyn.

One day not long after that a letter came to the Shoe offices from a Harvard doctor, a Dr. Dill, who expressed an interest in testing Jock in his fatigue laboratory as a "specimen."

Jock weighed 150 pounds stripped. Wires were attached over his heart, diaphragm, and at two points on his back. The machine, which resembled an escalator, was switched on and Jock performed: first the speed was set at four miles per hour, and he ran for five minutes. His pulse rate rose to 120 beats per minute during that test. Then he had his nose clogged with a gadget. Following a ten-mile rest, he ran again for five minutes while the machine was kicked up to seven miles per hour. The machine was sloped, which simulated uphill running, much as some of the treadmills do today. After another rest, his pulse registered fifty beats per minute, which Dr. Dill characterized as "extremely fit."

Jock said he could have told him that without all the torture. Worse, they didn't pay him, but he did get to sit at a table with a group of Harvard boys and eat as many potatoes and eggs as he could.

The Olympic Games, however, eluded Jock again in 1936. This time he had his citizenship, but not the ability. One perk did remain, however. In 1937 DeMar got himself into a spat with the AAU over expense money. Six months earlier Jock's United Shoe team captured the team title again at Boston, while Jock himself finished ninth. But, he was tapped by the AAU to replace Clarence DeMar on the Pan American team.

The AAU claimed that DeMar had written a letter to the *Washington Star*, the sponsor of the Pan American trials, asking for expenses based on his performance in the race. The funny part of it was that Clarence had an image as a model amateur. He did, and Jock often said he'd defend DeMar to the last, but the truth was that DeMar wrote the letter. DeMar later told Jock that he was mad at race officials who had secured expensive accommodations for themselves while assigning runners to dormitories. Modern runners such as Bill Rodgers, four-time winner of the Boston and New York marathons and Don Kardong, fourth place finisher at the 1972 Olympics, both strong advocates for runners' rights, have nothing on DeMar when it comes to ventilating righteous spleen, as Jock often claimed in his clinic.

Jock took seventh place at the 1937 Pan American Games, which was held on the campus of Southern Methodist University in Texas. The marathon, the climactic event, was run at eight P.M. in an effort to avoid the heat. Fat chance. The course was a curious one-and-a-half-mile loop around the stadium and was lit by flood-lights. It was horribly hot. And, water was ever more conspicuous for its absence. Every time Jock passed a huge fountain at the entrance to the stadium, he plopped in and splashed about. He took a dozen dips and lost time, but he didn't die in reality.

◆

Also during this time Jock got married, and it is fitting that his feet played a role in his nuptials. He was dancing one night upon his return to Boston, and as he sat down to drink a glass of punch he found himself sitting next to a gorgeous Scottish girl. He knew right then that he was going to become her future husband.

"Hi," he said, but she didn't answer. Betty was shy, but Jock always said she was the most beautiful girl he had ever seen.

They got married in 1938 in Allston, a little town outside of Boston. For sentimental reasons, Jock asked the preacher to read their marriage vows while he and Betty turned toward a window that faced east. It was New Year's Eve, and at exactly seven P.M. (midnight in Great Britain) the couple said, "I do," as London's Big Ben chimed in Jock's mind's ear.

That was it for both 1938 and Jock's bachelorhood as he and Betty rang in 1939. It was to be a watershed year that brought him the second most important connection of his life, according to him.

"Things aren't going so well at Shoe," he told Walter Brown after his team finished second at the Nationals in 1939. "Some of the bigwigs aren't pleased that we didn't win, and I will not be part of an outfit that does not respect a man's giving a race his all."

Walter knew what Jock was talking about. "Whenever you're ready," Walter said, "the BAA is waiting," and with that Jock disbanded the United Shoe team. Shortly thereafter he regrouped the team under the banner of the BAA's Unicorn. Over the next few years Jock missed only one day of work due to running. Even when the team traveled to Yonkers, a distance of some two hundred miles, he'd pile everybody in the car on Sunday after the marathon, and they'd drive all night to get to work by seven A.M. Monday morning.

The new team did well, until Pearl Harbor was bombed in 1941 and World War II broke out for the Americans. Jock was working at the shipyard in South Boston, and as soon as the news about Pearl Harbor broke he took a run down to the local military recruitment office.

"Can't get in," said the sergeant at the desk.

"Why not?" Jock asked.

"Flat feet," the man said.

Jock looked down to find, by God, the man was right!

"Say, aren't you Semple, the marathon runner?" asked another sergeant.

"Yes, and I want to join the Gene Tunney program," Jock said. The Gene Tunney program was the Navy's physical education division. "I want to be in the Navy. These dogs have run almost a hundred marathons and they have carried me around the world the equivalent of two times. America's in the war now. I want to fight, and I won't take no for an answer. Besides, who's going to see my feet?"

"Let him in," the second sergeant said. "He looks like the kind who plans to die with his boots on anyway."

## Chapter Six

### "I love being in the thick of the action."
### -Jock Semple

AFTER JOCK COMPLETED HIS duties in the Navy in 1945, Win Green, trainer for the Boston Bruins, said, "Jock, anyone can rub his hands up and down a hockey player's back. Trainers like that are a dime a dozen. Go back to college, son. Get a sheet of paper. Become the real thing."

While lying on his back in Saipan, thumbing through a copy of a Boston paper, Jock found an article about ex-athletes who had made careers for themselves in sports. Jock had that idea, too, but knew he could never get into running as a track coach because he had never been to college. But, while stationed at Samson Naval base in Geneva, New York, he had helped drill the raw naval recruits, so he had experience. It was there he met Bill Kennedy again after many years, who suggested Jock use his experience to become a physical therapist.

Thanks to Win Green and his excellent advice, and Bill Kennedy's encouragement, Jock went back to school. Green sent him to Walter Brown, who had just created the Boston Celtics, and Walter called Boston University (BU) on Jock's behalf. Classes in the physiotherapy department had already begun for the semester, but Walter got Jock a job as a carpenter at the university while he waited to enroll for the next term.

Jock always had high praise for Walter Brown. Carpentry jobs at BU didn't pay enough for a married man to live on, so Walter arranged for Jock to complement his salary by picking up a couple of bucks at the Garden. Jock guarded doors, but Walter made sure he was assigned the doors that were located way up high and had little traffic, so he could bring a book to study at night.

"Wanderlust Walter" they called him. Walter's father, George V. Brown, helped create the Boston Marathon in 1897, and Walter's son, George, still shot the gun at the start of the 1980s. The Hopkinton area of Boston was picked in 1897 as the site for the start of the race, not only because the course from west to east into Boston resembled the Greek marathon course, but because George Sr.'s farm was out that way. When George Sr. died in 1937, Walter, at the age of thirty-two, became not only president of the BAA but also general manager of the Boston Garden and Boston Arena.

Walter, who died at age fifty-nine in 1964, was a promotional genius. He was also a very gentle man, as Jock recounted to his patients in his clinic. Certainly Walter was world-renowned as an international sports figure. Even before he succeeded his father at the arena, he had established a reputation for himself by coaching the United States hockey team to its first world amateur championship in Prague, Czechoslovakia, in 1933. In 1940, he was named president of the company that owned the Boston Arena and Boston Garden.

Over the years Walter conjured many successful promotions. It was his idea to bring winter sports indoors to the Garden, and he built a huge indoor ski jump that attracted the world's best skiers. In 1932 Walter discovered Sonja Henie while on a tour through

Sweden with his hockey team. Almost from the moment Henie performed for an American audience at the Garden, she was received as a star, and her name became a household word. Walter created the Ice Capades, and later created the Boston Celtics, which brought him so many disappointments in the beginning.

Ultimately, the Celtics became a monument to the man, but in the late 1940s Walter had to fight with Garden Corporation board members to keep them from folding the team. For five years the Celtics dripped red ink before Walter finally succeeded in luring Red Auerbach, and under his coaching the Celtics became the world champions. But in truth, the team survived only because Walter scraped the bottom of the financial barrel and purchased the staggering franchise from the disenchanted Garden directors, according to Jock.

Originally, Walter Brown had disdained "bounceball." He had been a Grade A hockey man exclusively. But after World War II he recognized people's desire for an indoor game that could carry them through the winter between the football and baseball seasons, and with characteristic intensity, he set out to build the National Basketball Association (NBA).

Walter often ended up on Jock's rubdown table after spending a long day upstairs on the phone with creditors. "How long do you think it's going to take basketball to go over in this town?" Walter was repeatedly asked by Jock's patients during that era, who were on the tables beside Walter. "Five years, four if we can come up with a George Mikan," Walter said as Jock applied the soothing oils.

George Mikan, an early forerunner of the Kareem Jabbar big man, played for Minnesota. It did, of course, take five years. And then Walter's plan only worked through luck of the draw that brought Bob Cousy to the Celtics.

While Jock was recruiting his BAA team, he made part of his living at the arena by taking the Celtics out for their pre-dawn run. Walter had just created the team, and since he couldn't afford a hotel for them, he kept the players bunked in the basement on cots. It was fitting actually, the Celtics couldn't draw even their mothers to a game, as Jock put it.

"Aww right, all you laggards!" Jock shouted into the players' gymnasium quarters every morning at six to wake them for a run around the Fens, the wooded area south of Kenmore Square in Boston. A great bunch of guys, but with 22 wins and 38 losses their first year, they became the NBA Eastern Division doormat, a niche they promptly retained for years.

A man named Chuck Connors played for the Celtics then. Chuck regularly climbed on Jock's rubdown table, and regaled him and other patients with Shakespearean soliloquies, as well as renditions of the song well-loved by salon-denizens, "The Face on The Barroom Floor." Chuck never asked for the infra red lamp on his sore knee. Instead, he had Jock point the ultraviolet at his face. "I have an audition," he said, which made no sense to Jock until Chuck moved to Hollywood. There he landed the title role on the long-running television western of the 1950s and early 1960s, *The Rifleman*.

◆

In 1950 the NBA team, the Chicago Stags, ran into a heavy financial burden and were forced to drop out of the league. The league decided to send their three top players (Max Zaslofsky, Andy Phillip and Bob Cousy) to the Knicks, the Philadelphia Warriors, and the Celtics. But, the teams couldn't reach an agreement as to who would get which player, so they dropped the three names into a hat. New York picked Zaslofsky, a local New York City kid; the Warriors got Phillip; and Boston ended up with Cousy. At that time, the Celtic brass wasn't exactly enamored of the choice. Little did they know!

Cousy spent his first year as a sub, but when he cracked the starting lineup he proved to be the savior of the sport. If ever there was a man made for basketball, it was Bob Cousy, according to Jock. Just over six feet tall, he had the physique of a six-foot-eight man with large hands and feet, and terrific upper legs. Still, his greatest asset was his peripheral vision. He had cat's eyes, Jock called them. Cousy could see action behind him that enabled him to make breathtaking behind-the-back passes.

In a typical Jock story, one afternoon Couz (as Jock called Cousy) came in for a massage to get loose for a game that night. "He fell asleep on one of my tables as another of my patients walked in," Jock said.

"Hi, Bob," the other patient said, but Couz didn't answer. The next time I saw this fella he told me he thought Couz was a snob. "Bob didn't say a word," the fella said.

I told him Bob was asleep.

"But his eyes were open," the fella reported, and I had to explain that Couz had protruding eyeballs that made his eyes look like they were open.

"Cat's eyes," I told the guy.

"Oh!" he said.

With all due respect to the great players down through time, including Cousy, Jock believed that Bill Russell revolutionized basketball. The Celtics won eleven world championship titles in twelve years, beginning in 1957, largely due to the efforts of Bill Russell. Russell had led the US Olympic team to a gold medal in the 1956 Olympics before he joined the Celtics, but from the moment of his arrival he introduced something new: the blocked shot. Russell made an art of pounding down the ball. Then he grabbed it and started the fast break, which became the Celtics trademark.

Jock also had some fun at the side of the court. At one game he got into a row with referee Jacko Collins, and the ensuing fracas brought publicity to a sport that was starving for it." The row happened in a game with Syracuse. The Celtics were leading by one point when referee Sid Borgia disallowed a Boston basket, and that set Celtic coach Red Auerbach off.

"Sid took no guff," said Jock, "and he slapped Red with a technical. Still, Auerbach wouldn't stop and Borgia threw him out of the game. After a to-do on the floor, Red left, and I entered. I stormed up to Collins and blasted him about the behavior of Paul Seymour, the Washington National's coach, asking why Seymour hadn't been thrown out for a similar argument earlier in the game. Jacko followed me into the dressing room at intermission where he grabbed me around the throat, Jock explained to his patients.

"Big John Kerr of the Nats picked Jacko off Jock-o," Jock said.

Jock was fuming, as he recounted it, and he began to yell at Collins through the referee's door. "You can't do that to me, Collins. You can't do that to me." But Jock was wrong. Yes, Collins could! Jacko opened the door and attacked Jock again, ripping off his shirt before the fight was broken up.

These lighter moments brightened Jock's days with the Celtics, and made the ten dollars he received palatable, he said. Jock got less than that for his efforts putting on the Boston Marathon though.

"Spell it Z I P," he said. "In those days we Garden employees did the work as part of our jobs. But don't let me kid you, I loved it, to be in the thick of things," he said.

Jock ran his final marathon when he was fifty years old, he told his patients, and for tradition's sake, he ran his last marathon in Philadelphia over the same Sesquicentennial course where he had run his first marathon in 1926. Since that day he limited himself to working marathons in an official capacity, he said.

"And trust me, *running* the Boston marathon is much harder than running the Boston Marathon," he said to his patients' delight.

And so began another chapter is the saga of Semple!

## Chapter Seven

*"'Johnny Kelley, sir. That's my name,' the boy said to me.
And I said to myself: say hello to the new generation."*
−Jock Semple

JOCK STOOD IN HIS clinic in white shoes that tennis great Jimmy Connors had pulled off his own feet at a match and given to him to go with his white pants and white t-shirt. He looked like a dentist, except for the sweat.

"The sweat I owe to you boys," Jock told his patients. "Everything else I owe to Walter Brown."

Walter Brown had set Jock up at the Boston Arena with his first clinic, and that in turn was to lead to Jock's tenure as a co-director of the Boston Marathon, a duty parceled to him as an employee of the arena and garden.

"Without the break Walter gave me (he paid for all my equipment, too) I never would have made it in sports after my running days had passed," said Jock. "I had no education, past a couple of years in high school, and my carpentry abilities had earned me twenty dollars a week during the Depression."

Words so true! Without Walter, Jock might have lived after age forty-five as he had before: hand to mouth. Walter took his daily rubdown from Jock after his hard work upstairs in the office, as previously related, and it was on a table during one of those sessions that Walter told Jock how he hoped to live long enough to see a BAA runner win the Boston Marathon. Jock didn't say anything, but he never forgot those words.

After the Boston Athletic Association clubhouse on Boylston Street was sold to Boston University in 1933, BAA club offices were moved across the street to a floor in the Lenox Hotel. Even that proved too expensive and Walter, who had become BAA president, moved the office to the Boston Arena on Saint Botolph Street, where he became general manager and president. By that point Walter had set Jock up with a physiotherapy clinic in the arena, and that room became BAA Central.

After the fire that destroyed the arena, everything moved over to the Boston Garden, including Jock's clinic which became not only BAA Central, but Marathon Central.

The troops at the BAA had thinned by that point. Besides Walter and Jock, the members could be counted on one hand. They included Will Cloney, the current president and BAA Marathon director, longtime officials R. H. Kingsley Brown and chief timer Ellery Kock, and Walter's brothers, Tom and George.

Will Cloney had become marathon director in 1947 as a favor to Walter. Jock became co-director, but Will was always the more diplomatic member of the team. Contrast their two reactions to Rosie Ruiz in the 1980 Boston Marathon. While Jock was screaming, "She's a cheat 'n a fraud 'n a phony!" Will calmly called a hundred witnesses.

Will Cloney was a gentleman, much the way Walter was. For years Will worked as a sportswriter and college professor, and was chair of the English and Journalism departments at Northeastern University. Later, he became sports editor of the *Boston Post*, where he remained until it folded in 1956. Keystone Custodian Funds snapped him up, and before long Will became a vice-president. He gets great credit for helping keep the marathon alive. He and Walter funded the marathon with proceeds from the BAA track meet at the Garden. That track meet succumbed to financial problems in 1971, but Will worked out an arrangement with Prudential Insurance Company to help cover costs for the Boston Marathon. In the early 1970s the Boston Marathon finish line was moved to a spot in front of the Prudential Building on Boylston Street, where it remained until the early 1980s. Today the finish line sits several blocks east on Boylston Street, in front of the Boston Public Library, the site once occupied by the BAA club house of old.

When asked why he had given so much time to the race, Will once said, "I think somewhere along the line in life you have to try to be helpful." He didn't tell the reporter, but Jock knew that Will took the job to lighten the load on Walter, and like everyone else on the committee, Will never took a dime.

Jock's BAA team continued to improve throughout the 1950s, and before long he was attracting the good young college kids. Enamored of Czechoslovakian runner Emil Zatopek's training techniques, the kids were engaged in mild rebellion against the training programs imposed by their college coaches. Jock often found them up in his clinic looking for training tips from him.

Zatopek, who was that era's most rugged individualist, struck a chord with many young runners after World War II. Zatopek employed no coach, and instead invented his own workouts. Reportedly, he even ran with a telephone pole on his back. This appealed to the kids, who, though they did not look like beatniks, nevertheless shared a certain affinity for anti-establishment characters of the late 1940s and early 1950s. Jock had a team, one that was improving all the time, but he did not have a true "star" as yet, a runner who could take the lead, both in a race and as a model for the other runners.

Then along came Johnny!

"Let me tell you about Johnny Kelley (the Younger)," said Jock to a patient, "as so much of the joy I've had in life came from nudging Johnny along toward success, sometimes against his will."

Jock employed a standard approach in recruitment efforts for his BAA team in the 1950s: he sought out a man's wife or girlfriend first. While the men were out on the course during a road race, Jock would take the lady aside.

"The great advantage to having a man run for the BAA is that my BAA boys come home tired after I'm finished with them," Jock would say to the lady. Usually this elicited a polite nod, but little interest. "After men get out of work . . . oh, you know the diversions that exist for a man today." Jock repeated his spiel each weekend in towns such as Haverhill, Belmont, and Somerville. "Some men don't come home at all," Jock added. "Soon after they get married they discover the gin mills, the elbow-bending, and soon their wives have to trek down to some dark men's bar in housecoats. Never with my BAA boys! They come home every night, very tired, my boys do."

If Jock got the ladies hooked on the elbow-bending, he didn't have to say anything more. He'd give them an application, which they'd asked for, and by the next race he'd find himself ready to fire the gun, as a dozen women ran up to him with completed forms for their husbands and boyfriends. Jock wore the biggest smile in those days as he loaded the gun and turned to glance at Fred Brown, who had interrupted an extended, if fruitless, pitch for his North Medford Club, using traditional methods of recruitment, such as dropping the names of running stars that meant nothing to the ladies.

A very young and handsome Jock Semple. Image courtesy of the estate of Jock Semple.

Above: Jock Semple's father and mother (Francis Semple and Mary Duncan Semple) in Clydebank, Scotland. Date unknown.
Below: Jock winning a fifteen-mile race in Clydebank, Scotland in 1923.
Right: Jock finishes seventh in the 1930 Boston Marathon.
All three images courtesy of the estate of Jock Semple.

Jock with his mother, Mary, about 1930. Image courtesy of the estate of Jock Semple.

Jock, far right, with other marathon stars at Rockingham Park on August 8, 1932. Image from the collection of Dennis Brearley.

Jock (standing at far left) with the Lynn "Y" Team bound for Baltimore in the 1930s. Image from the collection of Bob Reid.

John Kelley (the Elder,) right, battles Gerard Cote up Heartbreak Hill in the 1940s. Heartbreak Hill was named for Kelley by legendary *Boston Globe* reporter Jerry Nason following Kelley the Elder's "heartbreaking" second place finish in the Boston marathon to Tarzan Brown in 1936. Image from the collection of Jerry Nason.

Left: The cover of the mileage log that Jock Semple kept throughout his running career.

Right: A page from Jock's record book that shows the sixty-six marathons that Jock ran between 1926 and 1943.

Both images courtesy of the estate of Jock Semple.

Right: A year-by-year breakout of the 23,115.5 miles Jock ran throughout his lifetime.

Below: Jock with his first Clydebank Harriers trophy in 1920.

Both images courtesy of the estate of Jock Semple.

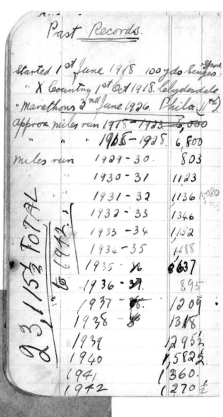

Past Records.

Started 1st June 1918   100 yds Singers Sports
" X Country 1st Oct 1918. Clydesdale
" Marathons 2nd June 1926. Phila (11th)
approx miles run 1918 - 1925   6,000
" " " 1925 - 1928.   6,800
miles run   1929 - 30.   803
" "   1930 - 31   1123
" "   1931 - 32   1136  1,080
" "   1932 - 33   1346
" "   1933 - 34   1152
" "   1934 - 35   1688
" "   1935 - 36.   637
" "   1936 - 37.   895
" "   1937 - 38.   1209
" "   1938 - 39   1318
1939   1295½
1940   1582½
1941   1360.
1942   1270½

23,115½ TOTAL to 1942.

Clarence DeMar winning one of his seven Boston Marathons.
Image from the collection of Jerry Nason.

Fred Brown, Jock's friend (and nemesis) racing in the 1930s. Image
from the collection of Fred Brown.

Jock (right) with A.L. Monteverdi in Philadelphia, 1934. A.L. ran and walked across the country in 79 days, 10 hours and 10 minutes: New York to San Francisco. Image courtesy of the estate of Jock Semple.

Jock (center row, behind #11) as trainer with First NBA Old-Timers All-Stars, 1957. Image courtesy of the estate of Jock Semple.

BAA Director Will Cloney (left) with Walter Brown, president of the Boston Garden/Arena Corporation. Image from the collection of Bill Wicklund.

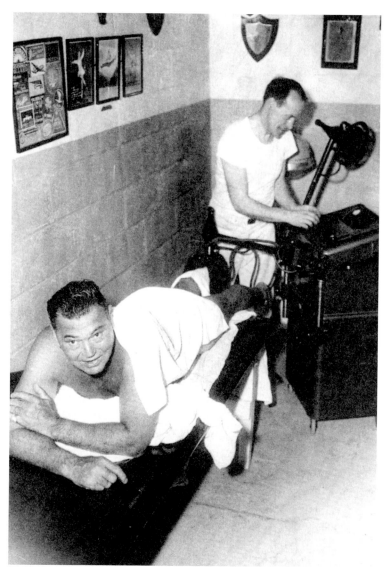

Jock gives heavyweight celebrity Jack Dempsey a "hotfoot" in the "Salon de Rubdown" in 1948. Image courtesy of the estate of Jock Semple.

Running colleagues from Jock's early days included Les Pawson
(left) and Tarzan Brown (right), both Boston Marathon champions.
Photos from the collection of Jerry Nason.

Jock and Betty Semple, 1940. Image courtesy of the estate of Jock Semple.

Image courtesy Leo White Illustrations.

"Good day for a run, isn't it, Fred?" Jock shouted as he sorted through his stack of applications, and the North Medford Club firebrand would glare at him.

"Tell us how you found your star," several patients asked.

It happened in Fall River, Massachusetts, on July 4, 1948, Jock explained.

"That day I met my star-to-be," he said. "But I didn't run that day, I went down to officiate—and recruit for my BAA team." His eyes adopted a far away gaze.

"Vic Dyrgall had been invited, so we brought down the best runners from Boston for the fifteen-kilometer road race, billed as the last major contest before John Kelley the Elder, Teddy Vogel, and Oli Manninen were to leave for the London Olympics."

Dyrgall had a rep as the best 10,000-meter man in America and nobody expected him to get beat, according to Jock. That is, until the race started and two high school kids shot out into the lead with Dyrgall, one boy on either side of him. The tinier of the two kids wore paper-thin track flats, the toes of which he had wrapped with adhesive tape after removing the spikes.

Neck and neck the two kids ran with Dyrgall until the tape on the thinner of the two kids' shoes began to unravel, and soon the shoes themselves disintegrated. Still, the thin boy ran, even as the shoes dropped off his feet in pieces, and by two miles he was running barefoot on the pavement under a 100-degree sun. By mile four his feet had worked themselves into bloody pulps.

Jock rode behind the lead group in his car watching as the two boys stumbled to the side of the road, the thinner one dropping out first. He was sitting in a ditch, picking pebbles out of his bloody blisters when Jock stopped to ask if the boy wanted a ride to the finish.

"Yes, sir, thank you, sir," the boy said.

"He was the most polite kid I had ever met in all my years in the running game," Jock said. "I was looking around for his girl-friend when I asked him what his name was."

"Johnny Kelley, sir," said the boy.

"And I said to myself as I thought of Fred Brown: *say hello to the new generation*."

◆

Johnny Kelley the Younger remembers meeting Jock from a differ-ent perspective.

"I met Jock formally one July evening in 1948 when, as a sev-enteen-year-old, I won both the place and time prizes in the Haver-hill Sons of Italy Ten-Mile Handicap Road Race. I ran after a not-so-auspicious debut in running a week earlier, where my shoes disintegrated and I dropped out," said Johnny the Younger.

"The Haverill Sons of Italy race was one week following my first race, where I had tried to match Vic Dyrgall. I fared better at Haverill, but was greeted with incredulity by most old-timers who could not fathom a seventeen-year-old winning the first race he ever completed. In the end, I relied on Jock's intercession to save me the prize and that's how I remember meeting Jock formally."

Johnny continued his tale, starting with his arrival at the Haverill Sons of Italy race on a train.

"Haverhill! Haver'll! Station stop is Hav'r'l!" the grizzled con-ductor twanged, dropping letters as the venerable coal-burning Boston and Maine locomotive decelerated. The train screeched to a halt. Seconds later I stood on the depot's cement platform as steam hissed from the idling engine, and sulfur dioxide belched in tropical blasts from the stack.

I had run two other road races in my life, finishing neither. A year earlier I had run at Littleton, Massachusetts, after traveling interminably on a bus with my father and my best friend George Terry. At that race I met John A. Kelley (later dubbed "the Elder.") I have always remembered the glow that flooded my father's face (whose name was also John), as the famous Kel turned to my dad before the starting gun and said to me, loud enough that my dad could hear, "You've got runner's legs kid."

Runner's legs notwithstanding, I did not finish that race nor my second one, a ten-mile run in Fall River the next year— and a week before the Sons of Italy race, where an older man with a Scottish brogue had picked me up and given me a ride after my shoes fell apart. At Fall River, George and I decided we had no strategy other than to run flat out and so we began the race by sprinting to the fore.

I ran shoulder to shoulder in scorching heat with Vic Dyrgall until, as noted, my shoes came unraveled. Then I ran barefoot and bloody. I had sent away for legitimate shoes from a mail-order house, but they never arrived. So I had taken a pair of my track flats, removed the spikes, and wrapped them around the toes with adhesive tape. First came the blisters, then came the unraveling tape, and finally the shoes burst. Soon I was relegated to a ditch before the kindly official with the Scottish brogue picked me up in his car.

On the day of the Sons of Italy a week later, George remained home in New London wearing an apron instead of a racing number. His supermarket boss loved sports, even profitless road racing, but Tuesday was always a big day in meats and green, and business, as his boss was wont to remind George, was business and the store shelves needed to be stocked—by George.

And so I was alone, because my father had died of viral pneumonia the previous December, and I've always regretted it that with his little-boy enthusiasm for running my pop died before getting a chance to see his son finish a road race.

Nevertheless, George and my poor dead Pop stepped along Haverhill's unknown streets with me as the sun started its decline on Tuesday, July 14, 1948. The outsized Rexall special wristwatch I had bought with the last of my paper route money jiggled at the end of my skinny arm. I held it to my ear. "Tick, tick . . ." Five after four.

I thought about never having travelled so far from home alone. Had it been no more than four years since a spoiled thirteen-year-old had run away to Springfield where his pop had come in the night to rescue him from the terrors of the city jail?

Soon, I came across two other fellas toting gym bags. They were much older, and wiser by the looks of them. "You guys runners?" I asked.

"Sure are, kid," said the darker-haired one, a guy with a George Raft face. "What's your name?"

"Kelley," I answered.

The other one, light-haired, raised a brow. "You sure picked a good name for this business, son."

"Did you ever hear of Johnny Kelley?" asked the first.

"I am Johnny Kelley," I said.

John A. Kelley, Johnny the Elder, the winner of the Boston Marathon in 1935 and 1945, had departed several days earlier on a boat for the 1948 Olympics. That I knew.

"Well . . .," the first man said, "if you're not playing a game with us on names, I'll tell you truthfully: I'm George Waterhouse, and he's George Pike. I run for the North Medford Club. Pike runs for Semple's outfit.

"And, believe it or not, we're friends," Pike added, clarifying nothing. What was the North Medford Club? And what was "Semple's outfit?

"Now," Waterhouse concluded, "since you're Johnny Kelley and you're not with the Olympic Team in London, you must be—"

"—another Johnny Kelley?" Pike scooped him. It was easy to see that the two were having a lot of fun at my expense.

"Yeah, I guess so," I said.

"Kid, in Massachusetts, you're either going to have to change your name or run like greased lightning," Waterhouse laughed.

"Probably too late to change my name," I said, resolute.

The second-floor hall swarmed with runners and I might have shorted out on the sight had not an electronic miracle transpired. In the far corner, mounted on a little stage, a bright picture box flickered and changed its image continually. Its magical revelation of a baseball game being played by the Boston Red Sox and the Washington Senators forty miles away momentarily blinded me to the splendor of eighty Vaselined feet and wintergreened calves.

"You won't run far watchin' that thing," a voice behind me chided as I stared at the box.

I turned to face a man with thinning brown hair and water-blue eyes. It was the same man who had given me a ride after blisters had forced me out of the Fall River Race. All my memory bank had on him was his bandy-legged shuffle and his unicorn-emblazoned jersey. Yet, he seemed to know me.

"Find yourself a chair an' get dressed," the man urged in a Scottish brogue so rich that I entertained by it at the expense of his meaning. "Where's yer sidekick?" he asked. "The other fella that put the scare into Dyrgall?

"Terry?" I said, "You mean George Terry?

"Yeah, I guess so," he said with a smile. "All Connecticut names sound alike. Te-irry, Ke-illy."

"George had to work today."

"Work?" the man asked, incredulous. "I didn't know runners worked." He leaned close, thumbing over his shoulder in a stagey confidence, "Most o' the' one I know are bums."

The object of his scorn, a man with a balding head, spun around and his words were loud, "Speak for yourself, Jock."

"I'm talkin' to this bright young fella, Fred Brown. Speak when you're spoken to."

Another runner nearby exclaimed, "Uh, oh, it's Semple and Brown. They're at it again."

Somebody across the hall yelled, "It's okay, Jock and Fred. We love ya both."

Jock (was it?) lost his fire as quickly as he had flared. "Listen," he said, "I'm goin' to see Mike Schena, the race director, and tell him this is your first race. What the heck? You still haven't finished one, have you? Ooh, I don't mean that as criticism. It's just that, in these handicaps, y'have to take advantage of every little assistance. Wait right here."

Soon he was back with a competitor's number.

"I got you five minutes. It should'a been eight, but with Kelley, Vogel, an' Manninen gone to London, everybody's been shoved down some."

He pinned the number to my shirt.

"Waterhouse and Pike'll be on scratch. What's NLOC?" he asked, pointing to my shirt.

"New London Olympic Club," I said, pride mixed with embarrassment. "I'm from New London. And I made the shirt with a marker."

His blue eyes twinkled. "Well, there's nothin' like settin' your sights high, lad."

He helped me pull the shirt over my head and get it on. "But don't you think one Johnny Kelley in the Olympics is enough?" he said, followed quickly, by "Of course you're a bit nervous today, but when you finish this race, you'll feel a lot better. And, believe me, there are goin' to be a few surprised faces at the finish line tonight."

"Yeah, mine especially," I said, "If I can finish this."

"Oh, fer cripes sakes! Those two races you dropped out of were just dress rehearsals. Tonight's your big performance, my boy."

Down on the street, Mike Schena blew his whistle, the hall emptied with many a clump and whoop and holler, and we were off! And the instant I finished I knew I had won both the time and place prizes. Somehow, when you do something right you know it, even if you have never quite accomplished anything of that magnitude before. So there I walked, chest puffed out, while all around me a carnival spun.

It was common in those days to finish races at the center of an amusement park. In this case we finished in front of a carnival on Washington Street. I wondered whether all the kids who jumped about could imagine why we pain-faced guys in numbered underwear staggered about coughing, wheezing, and swaying with our hands on our hips. The kids stared at us, while they continued to lick cotton candy or cadge a coin from their dads for one more ride on The Whip.

Also, handicap races were notorious for producing the slowest computation of race results imaginable. The Haverhill Sons of Italy would have been no different; that is, had not the man who had attended to me intervened.

The boom of Jock's voice came after twenty minutes of official hemming and hawing. One of the judges wanted to award the coveted Hamilton watch to Hawk Zamprelli, the veteran Somerville racer who had started on scratch. Another wondered whether George Pike had rightful claim to the watch. A third seemed to be trying to juggle the corrected times to drop my name lower in the ranking, where, he opined, "the kid" belonged.

Until that point, Jock had simply watched the proceedings. But when his voice thundered, it cleared the July air like a crack of summer thunder. "For cripes sake!" he roared. "This man, he clapped a fraternal/paternal palm on my shoulder, is unquestionably your time prize winner."

"What? The boy?" came a chorus.

"Use your noggin, man. Your head isn't just a hat rack. If he didn't win the time prize, how in the hell did he start five minutes ahead of your scratch man and finish seven minutes ahead of him? Answer me that."

A moment later, I wore the first-place watch. The prizes were awarded on the carnival grounds, under a square of a hundred or so sixty-watt bulbs, while the merry-go-round went oom-pah-pah and tired, cranky kids gooed up their cotton candy while their mothers and sisters tugged exasperatedly at their sticky hands.

Yet for me, this was an Olympic ceremony. Mike Schena stood straighter than Avery Brundage when he presented me with my two prizes, a huge trophy which I had undeniably won (no one could argue that I had not crossed the line first), and the Hamilton watch time prize, which, more coveted, would have been denied me but for the grace of Jock Semple.

Later that night I paused on the cement platform at the train station, much as I had stood hours earlier, but now I was a changed young man. Now I stood on the other side of the tracks possessing a trophy and a watch which indicated to me that I had crossed a new line, and in the dark I realized I no longer feared things as I had earlier.

Not only had I finished a race, I had won it! I had beaten the best of those who remained after the very best had left for the Olympics. There would be other days, and even bigger things to come, Jock told me.

But now all I could do was savor the moment. I stood waiting for the 10:09 local for Boston, where I would catch a connection for a train home to New London, Connecticut. I was only seventeen, and I missed my pop. But a whole new world had opened for me that day, and I had made a friend.

## Chapter Eight

"Go on up to Yonkers Sunday. A kid named Kelley's
running a marathon. See if you can make it interesting."
–An editor to a reporter

THE WORD MARATHON STILL put the word dance in the minds of
most Americans in 1963. The Boston Marathon had drawn fewer
than three hundred runners that spring, but the timing was right,
as editors at one of New York's daily newspapers sought to fill a
hole on the Monday morning sports page. This recollection of
events was a personal favorite of Jock's and if the years have di-
minished the accuracy of the quotes as they were passed along to
him, well so be it. Time does not diminish the pleasure that comes
with vindication.

"I've got eleven inches to fill," said the sports editor, as time
and again he and his reporters passed around a particular press release. "I keep getting copies of this release every other day. From
some guy, calls himself the coach-slash-trainer of the Boston Athletic Association marathon team.

"Coach-slash-trainer?"

"Yeah, also the father-slash-confessor, according to him.
Name is Jock Semple."

"Jock? I remember a Jock. A plodder, during the 1930s. He was the New England Champ three years, a pretty good plodder as I recall."

"What's a plodder?"

"A marathon runner. Bill Kennedy brought this guy Jock around to Portchester a few years back. Bill was coaching a bunch of kids, and I remember one time that Jock clipped a fire hydrant with his car while looking for a short cut to the race course. A wild man. Drove over the damn sidewalk."

"Jock says his BAA team is running in the National Championships at Yonkers on Sunday, and one of his kids, Johnny Kelley, the 'Younger' he calls him, is going for his eighth straight National Championship. I didn't even know they had national championships in that kind of running."

"Yeah, let's get the horse guy on it." He signaled across the room to a reporter in a rumpled suit. "Hey, what are you doing tomorrow at eight A.M.?"

"I was going over to Belmont. Check the action," the horse guy said.

"I've got action for you in Yonkers. The two-legged kind."

"Yonkers?"

"Yeah, go on up to Yonkers. A kid named Kelley's running a marathon. See if you can make it interesting."

I've got one problem. In terms of making that interesting."

"What?"

"Where's the drama?"

So the paper sent the horse guy to Yonkers to cover the National Championship Marathon. Johnny Kelley (the Younger) had won the race seven years in a row, an amazing and unprecedented achievement that has yet to be equaled. The paper figured something exciting must be happening in this sport, which formerly had attracted only thick-necked lumbering types, or so the general conception went.

The reporter, new to road racing, got lost and did not arrive at the start until two minutes after the gun had been fired. Quickly, he flagged the first official's car he could find, in this case an Oldsmobile with a handmade official's sign taped to the windshield.

"I let the man in and seated him in back beside Jerry Harvey, one of my BAA runners who had a sore throat that day," said Jock. "I had relegated Harvey to a job keeping oranges cut in quarters for Johnny. The driving I left to myself."

At one point, Jock rolled down his window to respond to a police officer who blocked the car at an intersection.

"Get out of my way, pleeeze," Jock shouted at the cop.

He wasn't mad, but he lagged behind schedule for meeting Johnny with a wet towel at five miles. Whether the cop heard or not, the reporter did. He saw too - chicken feathers flew and pedestrians scurried for shelter as Jock skidded the Oldsmobile around obstacles trying to get to Johnny at the ten, eighteen, and twenty-two mile marks.

Johnny won.

KELLEY WINS EIGHTH NATIONAL CHAMPIONSHIP IN A ROW, the *New York Times* headline read Monday morning. However, the article's subtitle said it all: BUT OHHH! WHAT A RIDE.

Drama discovered in the backseat of an Oldsmobile!

◆

"Jock was a larger than life character," said Bill Rodgers, who ran for Jock's BAA team for two years before his American record setting breakthrough at Boston in 1975. Still, being the best never insured immunity for anyone on the phone.

"I called Jock's clinic one day before Boston in 1975," Rodgers said. "I guess he didn't recognize my voice. He said something like, 'Get yer application, gotta qualify, and it's gonna be harder for ya to get in next year, so I don't want any more of yer guff.' Slam! And he hung up."

Rodgers first met Jock in 1973. Newly returned to running after college, he was introduced to Jock at a local race. "I didn't have a team to run for, but Amby Burfoot told me to mark BAA on the entry," Bill said. "Anyway, I got third and I guess somebody went up to Jock, and said, 'Hey Jock, your guy got third.' The next I knew this fella with a Scottish accent walked over to me. 'Who are you?' Jock asked. He told me that if ever I got an injury I should come see him at his Garden clinic."

Rodgers had laid off running for two years between 1971 and early 1973, and it happened that he got some kinks after starting again. He decided to give Jock a call.

"I went over to the Garden one day," Bill said. "I expected to find, you know, a clinic. Someplace that had carpet and enamel sinks. That kind of thing. Someplace to match Jock Semple's reputation as a famous former runner."

Bill knew the Jock legend. He knew that Jock, DeMar, Johnny Kelley (the Elder), and a host of other greats from the thirties used to ride in cars out of *The Untouchables* (the popular TV show from the 1960s about Chicago gangsters and the bootleg era) as they hiked up and down the East Coast to races. He knew all this, vaguely.

At first Rodgers couldn't find the room. "I think I walked around in a maze of dark corridors for about an hour. I expected to be knocked over by Jock's clinic. Instead, I found him in a tiny, tiny room way in the back of the Garden. He was working in an old t-shirt."

It was a normal day for Jock. He teased his patients about being overweight and they kidded him that he was getting rich off them. Rich? Jock threatened one corpulent customer that he was going to charge him for a man and a half.

"The phone kept ringing and guys hopped in and out of the steam bath," said Bill. "Jock moved others from the rubdown table to the whirlpool to the shower. Around and around."

All the time the phone kept ringing, which sent Jock scurrying to answer it. "Is there going to be a Boston Marathon this year?" one caller asked.

"There was a Christmas this year, wasn't there?" Jock said. And he hung up.

Jock turned to Rodgers, who stood in the doorway surveying the history on the walls.

"It was all up there," Bill remembered. "Many famous runners, and I stood in awe looking around it all."

"Yeah?" said Jock. "Whaddya need?" Rodgers had encountered the Jock tone for the first time in a personal way.

"I met you at the Silver Lake Dodge race a couple of weeks ago," Bill said. "Amby Burfoot introduced us. I got third, right behind Amby. You said I could join your team, that I should come see you. You said—"

"I said come right over, didn't I?" Jock flashed a robin's-egg blue-eyed smile.

"What?"

"I said come right over, not wait three weeks. Get on a table here. I'll move one of my men. Mickey, get up, will ya! Come on, fast, move it! This fella ran third at Silver Lake Dodge. Climb on, lad. Let's see what legs you have attached to ya. I've been bettin' people you'll be the next Johnny Kelley."

Time proved Jock right.

Johnny Kelley and his wife, Jessie, invited Bill to their house in Mystic not long after that. This was a year and a half before Bill set the American record at the 1975 Boston Marathon. His '75 run was the latter of two great performances that broke ground at Boston and advanced the marathon in America The other performance, of course, was by Kelley himself, who won the 1957 Boston Marathon and cracked foreign domination of the event.

The day the Kelleys had Rodgers to their home, Johnny and Bill trained with Amby Burfoot in New London. "Gutwrenchers," Amby called his workouts, a succession of all out miles and three-mile runs, designed to test mettle on a level that would have made Zatopek proud.

Amby is a key connection, because Kelley taught Amby in high school and coached him on the track team. Amby then roomed with Bill Rodgers at Wesleyan University and introduced Billy to Johnny Kelley.

In November of 1980, long after Bill had become marathon's golden boy, Johnny and Bill Rodgers sat down at Bill's store in Boston to compare the era in which each competed, and to reminisce about the contribution Jock made to each of their careers. Around them, customers at the Rodgers Running Center in Cleveland Circle bounced on one foot, then the other, testing shoes. Sweat suits were pulled off the rack and replaced. At one point, a baby was dropped into Bill's arms from behind, as the tot's proud mother sought to solicit a Rodgers smooch for her tiny charge.

"When I first ran for Jock on his BAA team, I took rubdowns after my workouts," said Bill. "I'd lie on the table as Jock told stories about the Boston Marathon. He'd work on me in that tiny, little room of his in the Garden when suddenly he'd rave about the clowns. He'd be furious. Jock hated imposters and frauds, you know. He only liked what he called the "real" runners. Some guy would have worn a cow head or something during the race, and that would get him started."

Bill ran for Jock for nearly two years. The BAA runners were scattered about Boston when he joined Jock's team, so he trained with runners out near Jamaica Plain. When the Greater Boston track club was created, many of those runners joined Greater Boston, and Bill left the BAA to join the new team.

"I don't think Jock minded," Bill said. "We remained good friends and he told me he understood. He had a big thing about going for the opportunity, you know, and that's what he told me. Jock was always very supportive of me. I remember I was in the car with him one time. We had Charlotte Lettis, the top woman running in Boston at the time, in the car and Jock started to defend himself. He told her he didn't hate the women. I was new and didn't know him very well. He was talking to Charlotte, but really to me, to convince me that he wasn't evil.

"Making the comparison, Bill, you took rubdowns from Jock, and he offered you encouragement when you were brand new to the marathon," said Johnny. "That was the case with me back in the 1950s. There were times when I lived in places other than Boston, but I found even then that Jock exerted a very strong influence over me, despite any distance. I had the feeling he was there, even when he wasn't."

Bill said, "Jock was a great influence at the races, but I met people who said he created havoc at the start of the Boston Marathon, you know, when he waved his arms and shouted. But that was his charisma. Jock was a great runner himself, and loved the game.

"I once saw Jock throw a guy at the starting line who wasn't supposed to be there," Bill said. "The guy was in his thirties and wore a very high number, and Jock was about seventy. He just picked the guy up and threw him back. Pretty amazing, but I'm happy Jock did that. The runners have to be honest, you know, and if you haven't qualified, then you should go to the back of the pack. You have to go where you feel you can run and everything, but don't get up with the top runners where you might cause a collision and get people hurt. Everybody's got to work together on that."

"Jock was sort of the enforcer," commented Johnny.

"Right," said Bill. "But sometimes top runners won't say something to someone who is out of place. I know I wouldn't. If I had a ten-year-old kid come up next to me or some runner with a number that didn't belong there, I'd be hesitant to say anything. But not Jock.

Bill remembered another funny story, when he saw Jock jump into the Boston Marathon during the middle of the race. "I was running at the front and some guy on a bike came in close to me and Jock appeared. Well, he took the handle bars and drove the guy right back into the crowd."

After the race in 1975 when Bill won Boston, Jock called him up to his clinic. Jock said he had a special award for Bill from the Mexican team. Bill went up and Jock presented him with a block of wood about six inches by six inches with a plaster of Paris dog head on top of it.

"It was the most bizarre award I had ever seen in my life," said Bill. "But that's the type of award or memento Jock had scattered around in that tiny room of his."

In 1975, Jock ran out beside Bill in the last stages of the Boston Marathon to offer encouragement. "Get goin,' lad," said Jock. "They can't catch ya even if they had roller skates!"

When Bill finished the race, an AAU official told him that had Jock given him water, or anything else at all, he could have been disqualified. It was so backward back then. Bill remembered the official really coming down on him, saying that he had received coaching during the race.

That kind of thing was true in Johnny's time as well. "The AAU always had that rule," he said. "But Jock had a defense, he told them he wasn't helping just one runner, he was helping everybody. And he did. He never held water back. He gave water to his runners, but he gave it to the guy next to you also. He told me this year, though, he could no longer do it. I don't know whether he meant he could no longer do it officially, or whether the crowded conditions prevented him."

"Probably the crowds," said Bill. "Was it easier, less crowded, in your time?"

"Well, here's an interesting thing," said Johnny. "I remember Boston being immensely crowded. But recently I went up to the attic to dig out a box of old clippings from the year I won, and I found somebody had taken a photo of the start from a rooftop, and I couldn't believe the difference. Maybe a million people stood on the sidewalks watching that day, but we had only 140 runners in the race in 1957."

"As a front runner, of course, you wouldn't notice that. I mean you wouldn't notice the difference, I'm sure."

"It's true that you always run against the people you know are the top competition," Johnny said. "It isn't really the numbers; you're right. But, you have an uncanny ability to tune all that out and just run your own race. I mean the crowds. I think if I had to compete at the top level today, I'd go sneak off in the woods to cope with the pressure. I felt the pressure, Billy, I did!"

"Didn't you have the feeling though, that you wanted to get to the finish line just so you could hear again?"

"I wanted to get there, but I didn't get there in two hours and nine minutes the way you did."

"You went to the front, though," said Bill. "You didn't hang back off the pace and wait for the others to collapse. You battled them right at the front."

"In my time, yes."

"But all times are slowly coming down. I'll tell you an interesting story. In 1975 I got an invitation to Holland. I had just started getting expense money. As you know, you have to make a breakthrough before you get anything—money, gas, anything. So, I had an opportunity to go to Holland and have my expenses paid. 'Go for it,' Jock told me. 'Take the money.' I think Jock understood. In a way I think he wanted runners to make money. He was a great runner himself, and he understood what it meant to be an athlete. But he had tradition to think about at Boston."

At the time of the conversation between Bill Rodgers and Johnny Kelley (the Younger) there was talk of a grand prix type of competition, with races all over the world, and there was talk of including Boston. But Jock and Will Cloney never bent to pressure. They wanted to develop things on their own, and when they made their decision, they did it their way.

"You know, I think of Jock as a Muhammed Ali type of character," said Bill. "He's great with the press. He's a good talker and a good speaker. He's still so excited about running. That's how I think of Jock, as somebody who will always love running."

"No matter how much the game changes."

"It's amazing how things have changed. And keep changing."

"Times change," said Johnny, "but Jock changed too. Yet he never changed. I was talking to someone who ran for him in the 1930s on his Lynn Y team. To listen to the guy tell the stories, it was the same Jock I knew. That you knew."

"And that Patti Catalano knew. He helped her tremendously. She told me I should start taking rubdowns again. Jock promised to take two minutes off my next Boston time. I'm thinking of going up. Two minute, phew! I meant to ask, were you in college in 1957 when you won?

"I graduated in 1956," said Johnny.

"So you were what, about twenty-three?"

"No, I had been in the army and came back out to finish my last few college courses. I was twenty-six when I won."

"Isn't that bizarre? When someone is only twenty-two years old, like Roberto Salazar, and they win New York and Boston?"

"Of course when you're thirty-three and you've done it as you have," said Johnny, "when you have proved yourself as long as you have, that's the great trick. A kid can come along at twenty-two, but there's no telling how long he can maintain. Can he do it for ten years? I don't know. I had guys like that. They burst on the scene and I was threatened, but then they'd be gone. We'd never hear from them again. I think that's the challenge, to stay at the top, and you've proved that.

"One last question, Johnny. What was your weather like in 1957?"

"Perfect."

"Not too hot? I hate the heat."

"Perfect. Sunny, with a breeze. And sixty degrees."

"Hey," said Bill, "what's this? Is this a baby? Where did this baby come from?"

"Can you sign his bib?" asked the mother. "We promise to save it."

◆

Jock may have changed with the years, but he never mellowed, as is seen in this 1971 column.

JOCK THINS MARATHON BY INTUITION

by Tim Horgan *Boston Herald American*, April 13, 1971

The telephone rang and Jock wrenched his fingers from Boston Bruin John McKenzie's pelt and leaped to answer it.

"Hey!" yelped McKenzie, "Jock get back to work. I've got a playoff game tonight."

But even the Bruins run second to the BAA marathon this week, five days before the 1971 race, at least in that rumpled corner of the Garden known as J. Semple's Salon de Rubdown and Bunion Removal.

This, as usual, is Marathon Central. The phone screams incessantly, grown men in short pants trot in and out, regular customers lie fallow on the rubbing tables and the maître d' himself is everywhere at once.

"This is the worst it's ever been," said Jock for the umpteenth year in succession. "It's those bloody ten-milers."

Just in case anybody here is *not* running in Monday's marathon, the entry rules have been changed somewhat since last time. To get into the act, a chap must either:

1. Have run a marathon in three and a half hours or less, sometime or other. (One of this year's entries last did it in 1955.)

2. Or have run ten miles in 1:05, fifteen miles in 1:45, or twenty miles in 2:30 within the past year.

"*You* could run ten miles in 1:05," Jock accused one of his customers. "But it would take you ten *years* to run another sixteen. Yet we've got to take these guys in, even the halt and the lame, as it says in the Bible."

Some people think the BAA has become too discriminating, that the fame of this race lies in the garden variety of its field. Jock is not among them. And since he's also in charge of weeding out the unqualified, it's no wonder Monday's starters will total only nine hundred, compared to last year's 1112.

IBM and Honeywell reportedly are vying for rights to Jock's method of screening applicants.

How do you do it?

"First, I read *Runner's World* to get the results of races these guys claim to have run in," Jock said.

Then?

"Than I use my intuition."

How?

"Easy. I get suspicious. If someone says he ran 3:29, I get suspicious. That's how I caught three kids lying."

Jock peered around the room and lowered his voice to a conspiratorial bellow. "They were from Notre Dame, shame on them." Jock peered skyward, looking for thunderbolts.

But, there was a chap from Australia who claimed he'd run three marathons Down Under within the prescribed time. Jock couldn't verify it; but he let the guy in anyway. How come?

"I could tell he's honest."

How?

"He *looks* honest," said Jock, who's never laid eyes on the bloke.

Nonetheless, Monday's field will be the usual representative one, led by No. 1 John Kelley the Elder and No. 2 John Kelley the Younger, who's now forty. There will be the two Finns, five Central Americans and an Englishman for foreign flavor. And there'll be what Jock terms a "literary battle" between authors Erich Segal (*Love Story*) and Hal Higdon (*On the Run from Dogs and People*).

Jock also let in two priests shortly after he tossed out the lads from Notre Dame.

The race itself, however, is a mere formality. "There's no doubt who'll win," said Jock. "Pat will. Pat McMahon."

This is the twenty-nine-year-old Lowell school teacher from County Claire, Ireland. How can he lose?

Can any American-born entry win?

"Oh, sure," said Jock. "He can win first American."

A stirring from the rubdown table: "Has the game started yet?" mumbled McKenzie. "I've got the playoffs tonight."

## Chapter Nine

"Hey, Jock this K. fella number 261 looks pretty good.
What's her mother call her, Jock, Karl?"
–Newspaper reporter

A PATIENT, THE ONE from the hot box who had returned to the clinic for another day and another treatment (and to the hot box, his special perch from which he loved to bait Jock) asked, "Anything burn you more than the phone, Jock?"

"Oh, cheats and those who commit skullduggery!" said Jock. Whenever I speak at a runner's convention, I'm always asked to address myself to cheating in the Boston Marathon.

"Events by one Rosie Ruiz in 1980 (everybody knows she is no lovely flower to me) have grabbed the headlines. But actually, cheats have always been a thorn in my side. In 1935 I was asked to put on a marathon, the Lawrence to the Sea race. It was an ordeal because of the cheats, and I wouldn't recommend administration to anyone except those who own an Excedrin factory.

"There was a fella in that race that was a brazen cheat. I passed him at the start and did not see him again until the two-mile stretch before the finish line. Then I saw him in front of me. Imagine my surprise! I ran hard and I beat him, but when I crossed the line I spun around, pointed my finger, and called him a cheat. I reported him to the referee, but the checker at the twenty-mile mark had left his post after the leader passed and the referee would not take my word. So I grabbed the nearest microphone.

"'This man is a cheat,' I announced during the award ceremony. 'By finishing in the silver medals he has robbed another man of his silver medal. Instead, that man got a bronze.'"

"Still nobody listened. Finally, I shouted, 'I hope it happens to you someday.' Then I found the 21st man and I gave him my silver medal and took his bronze.

"There were numerous occasions in the Boston Marathon when people cheated, but they were never serious enough to affect the prize list. I had a number of athletes tell me that during the marathon they saw number such and such come out of a car. It is impossible to correct every instance of this, of course, but thankfully most runners are sportsmen and sports ladies," he said.

In terms of women, Jock was in great favor of women running—when they did it legally, which according to him Kathrine Switzer did not do (as he has always contended) and that prompted the "Great Shoving Incident," as it has been called. The incident occurred a mile or so outside Hopkinton after the start of the 1967 race. In those days the press bus started behind the runners and wound its way through the crowd to the front.

Suddenly one of the newspapermen shouted, "Hey, Jock," he called, "you've got a broad in your race." Nobody ever accused Boston sportswriters of being demure.

"At first nobody believed the newsman," said Jock, "because the year before we'd had a scare. A half-mile out of Hopkinton a group of newspapermen had shouted, 'Hey, Jock, a broad!'

Nobody ever accused Boston sportswriters of being overly creative either.

"I had the driver pull up close and we all leaned in for a look. False alarm. It was a boy with long hair. He had the shoulder length variety, but still he was a boy. There are ways you can tell, ya know.

"Then in the 1967 race somebody yelled again, "Hey, Jock, this time it is a gal. And holy smokes she's wearing one of your numbers.' You would have thought the bus would tip over with everybody hopping up to see and sure enough, it was a girl. And, she was wearing one of my official BAA numbers! Co-conspirators. The thought occurred to me instantly that the young lady must have had some scoundrels providing assistance. How else could she have gotten a BAA number?

"In 1967 all runners were required to take a physical exam at the starting line. Doctors put the runners through a test. We conducted the test like the army, you know. The men lined up and the doctors say, 'Cough.' Now the doctors couldn't very well say to a woman, 'Cough.' Could he? And have her slip by undetected?"

That's what made Jock suspect this young woman had used subterfuge, most likely with the aid of co-conspirators. She wore the number 261, and Jock grabbed a program from one of the newspapermen. K.V. SWITZER, the program read.

"Ah," said Jock, "just her initials! She had tricked me by sending an application with only her initials instead of her first name. I used to assign the numbers for the Boston Marathon between periods of the Bruins and Celtics games. Bobby Orr must have had an outstanding game for me to miss that one, I thought. In any case, I had to deal with so many cheats, no wonder my eyes had begun to go batty. Still, I kicked myself for my mistake. But of course the newspapermen were having their fun."

"Hey Jock, this K. fella, number 261, looks pretty good," one said.

"What's her mother call her, Jock, *Karl?*" said another.

"You know how the newspapermen are," Jock said, "and the bus rocked with laughter. I've got a theory about newspapermen. Their love for exaggeration is exceeded only by their affection for window seats on the press bus while Jock Semple is out on the street trying to save the honor of the Boston Marathon."

This was the second time a woman had snuck into the race. The year before, Roberta Gibb, a university student, hopped out of the bushes at the start and ran the race. Jock saw her but didn't chase her. She didn't have a number. That had been Jock's point all these years: She wasn't cheating by using subterfuge.

Roberta Gibb ran the race in 1966 in three hours and 29 minutes. All the newspapermen had already filed their stories, beautifully written articles about Kenji Kimihara of Japan and Kimihara's courage as he led three other Japanese runners for a sweep of the first four places. Kimihara wasn't supposed to have posed a threat to his teammates, particularly Toru Terasawa, but he put on a fine sprint at the end, into a twenty-mile per hour headwind, and won the race in the last two miles. Very exciting. But, the newspapermen all had to dump their stories when a kid ran up out of the garage under the Pru at three-thirty and shouted, "Holy cow, a girl finished the race!"

"The news upset one fella in particular and his face dropped, like a bus tire going flat," said Jock. "He had just finished telling everybody how his story on Kimihara's victory that day made Shakespeare look like a four-hour man. Worst of all, the poor fella didn't even favor women golfers."

But now, in this race, number 261 was real, and she was wearing an official BAA number, which meant Jock, protector of the rules, had a problem.

"Hey, Jock," somebody shouted. "What are you gonna do about K.V. Switzer?"

There was no question that Jock intended to deal with her as an interloper, and he told the driver to stop the bus. Jock was pretty famous in those days already—or infamous rather—and all the newspapermen knew him as someone who could be relied upon to save the marathon from mockery, which is how he perceived this case.

One year, Jock had jumped in after a man broke through the barricades to run the last 200 yards with the leader. The man saw Jock and ran like hell. They both beat the leader across the line as Jock chased the man through the crowd and into the lobby of the Lenox Hotel. The man kept running and Jock chased him down into the basement before he cornered him at the end of a corridor and wailed on him. Jock booted the guy in the behind and pulled a muscle in his leg for his effort. He lost a week's pay when he couldn't run the Celtics around the Fens.

In 1967, though, Jock couldn't get off the bus to chase Kathrine because Will Cloney stood in the well in front of the door. This was Will's customary position. He stood there so he could direct the motorcycle policeman, but he also stood there to keep Jock from chasing people.

"I wasn't going to harm the young woman," said Jock. "I just wanted my number back. This was an innovation, a woman in the Boston Marathon. But it was also subterfuge and I looked at it as 'my' number because I had given it to her by mistake.

"Everybody has been confused all these years over this next point," Jock continued. "After the bus stopped, Will hopped off first. Later, when a newspaperman asked me for an interview, I made the statement, 'Will was too slow to catch her,' because Will ran after Kathrine first, but he did not reach her. Don't listen to any of those stories by so-called authorities who try to tell you that Will was still on the bus. I'm telling you the truth here. Will missed.

Then I got off the bus to give it a try. I started running and I caught up to the young woman and her gang of co-conspirators pretty quickly. They were a close-knit bunch of scoundrels, her co-conspirators with her, still I slipped through the mob and reached in for my number, to grab it back.

"Again, the story has snowballed. The fact is the guy who slammed into me wasn't that big. Bigger than me, certainly. But not as big as the Pru, as some newspapermen would have you believe. Anyway, some big bruiser butted in. He later became Kathrine's husband, but that doesn't change the fact that he wasn't much of a football player, that he couldn't knock down an overworked old man.

"That is another point I have to clear up. Today the younger newspapermen have begun to exaggerate on the exaggerations. Some of them will tell you that I got knocked over the telephone wires. Others will say Jock Semple went flying across the road into the bushes. And the worst of all, one cub reporter wrote last year that the fella knocked me on my ass. Now I'm asking all you honest people, so we can set the record straight, don't give these liars so much credit."

One thing is true, however. A photographer snapped the whole sequence of Jock getting off the bus, chasing Kathrine, reaching for the number, the whole episode. Even the *Stars and Stripes*, the official newspaper of the US Army, had the seven pictures of the sequence the next day.

"I started getting ribbed from Guam," said Jock. "Worse, my wife Betty fed the dog roast beef and I ate Swanson's. But take a good look at those pictures. Not one of them shows me going over telephone wires, does it? So listen to me. It's true the guy did block me. But this is the God's honest truth, the way it happened. I tripped over my shoelace the instant before he hit me."

Jock went on to tell the story about Rosie Ruiz. "That has to be the most flagrant example of skullduggery," he said. "I don't put Rosie on the same level with Kathrine. Kathrine is a true athlete. She might have been guilty of subterfuge, but at least she trained for her run. This Rosie, however, she'll get no bouquet from me. She ran a so-called marathon at New York the year before, according to the reports. Then she supposedly ran at Boston and supposedly ran the second fastest race ever by a woman. Actually, her improved time at Boston speaks more for the speed of the Boston transit system compared to New York trains.

"Maybe you think I'm being too hard on Rosie. I certainly am. She swindled Jackie Garreau, the real winner, out of something irreplaceable. I don't care how many motorcades they give someone the week after, the fact remains that nothing can replace the cheers that are offered an athlete who has sacrificed so much for that one day. That is what Rosie stole from Jackie in 1980 by jumping into the late stage of the race ahead of her. She stole the cheers of the crowd as much as she stole the gold medal with the diamond stud."

After many investigations Rosie Ruiz was eventually disqualified from the Boston Marathon, and New York also disqualified her. Officials were able to prove that she did not run the complete course.

"To my mind she left the subway in New York and walked to the race's rest area where she lay down on a cot and someone took her computer number and put it on the spindle," said Jock. "Whether it was a friend or a gung ho minor official we will never know. In the future we will guard against these things. We will be more careful to check the ladies as well as the men at various checkpoints during the race, but to me we have done a good job in past years for both the men and women. I think Rosie didn't intend to finish up so high. I think she just wanted to please her employer, who had given her expense money back in New York and sent her to Boston. After her bogus 2:56 time in New York she couldn't very likely run a six-hour marathon, could she?"

Jock was at the finish line when Rosie finished with a bad case of the staggers. She gasped, "All I wanted to do was finish."

"I didn't know who she was," Jock said, "but I heard someone on the loudspeaker say 'Congratulations, Mrs. White,' and I thought she might be Jennifer White, who is married to one of my former BAA runners, Max White. I rushed over to congratulate Rosie thinking she was Jennifer White, and Rosie looked at me like I had two heads, and neither one screwed on correctly.

"That's when Fred Lebow came over to me and said, 'We don't know her either, Jock.' That set me off and immediately I called her a cheat and a fraud. You wouldn't believe the 'recovery' she made in the garage below the Pru, especially as she had no sweat on her. I got some criticism for my remarks as the news hounds with the mikes picked up my calling her a cheat. Later, an ambulance chaser wrote to Cloney and said I should be thrown off the race committee and I should be sued. But soon the evidence poured in and I was proved correct, even to the thief allegations. As you know, Rosie refused to return the medal that was rightfully won by Jackie Garreau, which to my mind made her stunt a travesty.

On the point about qualifying times, where Boston has a qualifying time of 2:50 for men under forty, Jock said, "I won't go into why we need qualifying times except to say that we will drop them the day God makes the roads bigger out of Hopkinton."

Jock was always suspicious of race promoters across the country who gave certificates to runners with 2:49:9 times. One glaring example of this happened in 1979 in Lowell, Massachusetts. The marathon was scheduled the day after Boston entries closed. Jock asked Will Cloney if he could give those runners a few days' grace. He said okay, and Jock advised the runners who qualified at the Lowell race to get their certificates photocopied the next day or deliver them personally to Jock at the Boston Garden.

"Now listen what the officials did," said Jock. "As every last runner crossed the finish line, officials handed out blank certificates and told the runners to fill out their time and place themselves. A brilliant idea from someone with a vacant head! I know this much. I never saw so many marginal times in my life in all categories. The day of the Boston Marathon the sun had been down for hours and here were jokers still pouring across the line —all wearing my official numbers."

Jock buried his face in his hands that day. He couldn't bear to see a thousand cheats pouring across the line.

The hot box guy was kind enough to call attention to the fact that Jock had his face in his hands, even in the telling!

## Chapter Ten

*"I run until I can't run anymore. And then I run some
more," he crowed. You could see the little boy's love for
a game he had learned to play better than any
other little boy in the world.*
–Emil Zatopek

JOHNNY KELLEY (THE YOUNGER) was hopelessly confused by the
Jock Semple/Fred Brown feud. Twenty years old and new to
Boston, he had been told by Jock to avoid Fred Brown, who surely
would attempt to "steal" him for the North Medford Club. Fred
was dictatorial, Jock said.

On the other hand, Fred told Johnny to avoid Jock. "The
man's a nuisance," Fred advised the boy. "He's got no control over
his temper. His wife tells him he should calm down. He should be
like Fred Brown, his wife tells him. But that only gets him angrier.
The man is positively dictatorial."

But Johnny Kelley liked Jock, he commented to Fred.

"You've gone soft in the head," Fred Brown said, looking for
all the world like Henry Miller mimicking a Boston book censor.

"Kel isn't really soft, Fred," Johnny's friend Chris McCarthy
interjected. "Just loyal."

"To the wrong cause!" Brown exclaimed. "That Scotchman will soon have you running in a tartan. You won't even get to wear green on Saint Paddy's Day if you stick with the BAA."

Johnny feigned ignorance. Still, he knew that Fred and Jock, both former great runners, had become not only major domos of the two top runners' clubs in New England, but they also continued their bitter rivalry. In 1951 Johnny was a new runner in Boston, on scholarship at Boston University. He was twenty years old, bursting with enthusiasm for school, running, and for life. Here, Johnny picks up the telling of the story.

Some success had come my way in running since I had met Jock at the Sons of Italy race in Haverhill in 1948, and after receiving many letters from him, I joined the BAA. My choice irritated Fred Brown, who came to Chris McCarthy's house one night for dinner, presumably, to "save" me.

"Maybe I am a bit soft, Fred," I said. "But what's so bad about running for Jock?"

McCarthy shot me a look and said, "You asked for it, kid, get ready."

"Bad?" Brown rolled his eyes toward the ceiling. He passed an incredulous palm across his billiard ball dome. "My God, man, it's not bad. Just damn foolish, son. Who's going to care for young Johnny Kelley when his legs give out from racing in every burg from Boston to Kalamazoo to win trophies for Jock's physiotherapy parlor? Who'll go out for Saturday jaunts at eight minutes a mile with young Kelley when he can't run any faster?"

"I can't guess, Fred. Who?"

"Well, me and Old Chris here, and Dave Gott, and all the other good old boys from North Medford, that's who."

"What about the good old boys of the BAA?"

"I can't believe you, Kelley. I do believe your ancestors hailed from Cork. Thick as oak. The BAA stands for Be An Ace! When you're not an ace any more, Semple won't want you. North Medford means Nice Men."

It was an old dialogue in a new setting. Ironically, Chris McCarthy, who had cast his running lot with Brown and North Medford, lived within half a block of Jock's physiotherapy parlor at the decrepit Boston Arena.

Brown tried to forget this proximity as three of us sat in Chris' apartment on Saint Botolph Street. It was enough to realize that Jock's own "open arms to runners" policy extended to Brown's boys too. The good ones anyway. Rising North Medford stars like Dave Gott frequently joined Jock's boys on their Saturday treks from the arena to Jamaica Pond and back for such BAA blandishments as free rubdowns.

Fred Brown winced to picture that Saturday scene. And now Chris McCarthy, bunked so close to Jock's den, might slip into it. Luckily, the spaghetti had finished cooking, and McCarthy placed a steaming plate between Brown and the vision of Jock's Sabbath corrupting his innocents.

As the wine appeared, Brown brightened. "Did I ever tell you guys about the race. Oh, God, it was hot. We were broiling, Jock and I battling it out, stride for stride, right down Somerville's main street, no shade, out thirteen miles, two to go. Well, much as I couldn't stand the thought of the old Scotchman beating me (of course he was maybe a young Scotchman then) I just couldn't take that heat another step, when, lo and behold, I spied a tier of tonic crates on the sidewalk. I told Jock, 'So long, good luck,' and stopped to swig the contents remaining in every one of those bottles. There must have been a hundred, all drunk out of and ready to be sent back to the plant."

"Well?" we said.

"Well, what?"

"Did you recover and catch Jock?"

"Nope. I never saw the Scotchman again that day. Of course, he didn't sweat like I did. Being Scotch, he wouldn't waste the water."

Brown could twist a tale, all right, and I wanted to keep him twisting. "Can't you think of anything you have in common with Jock?"

Slowly the incredulous hand passed again over the pate. "Not one hell of a lot. But I will concede this: Jock used to be a vegetarian. That he gets points for."

"How's that?"

"For one, I'm a vegetarian. You see I once worked in a stockyard, and let me tell you, that's enough to make Henry VIII a vegetarian. So, if I have to say something good about Jock, that's it."

"That's all? No other good points?"

"Well," Brown frowned. "There probably are, but if I told you guys, you'd think I was getting soft on Semple. But listen, while I've got you, did I ever tell you the goat's milk story?"

◆

When Jonny Kelley entered Boston University in September of 1950, Ernest Hemingway was being praised for his novel *Across the River and into the Trees*. The lion of mid-century American literature was two years away from his last acknowledged gem, *The Old Man and the Sea*. Eleven years short of suicide.

The New York Yankees had dominated the American pastime from the beginning of time. On the pop music scene, Mario Lanza's "Be My Love" dueled with Nat King Cole's "Mona Lisa," while a skinny, tormented country boy named Hank Williams rode in style from town to town, stretched out and strung out in the back seat of his custom Caddy. Lefty Frizzell sometimes nudged him on the charts, but nobody was going to beat the composer of "Your Cheatin' Heart."

The Korean War was three months old.

Joanie Porter was Johnny's girlfriend back in Groton, Connecticut. Her mother called Wisconsin Senator Joseph McCarthy, the Communist hunter, "a great patriot." Paul Memos, Johnny's roommate in the Myles Standish Dormitory, called McCarthy "the scum of the earth."

Johnny argued with Joanie's mother and helped Paul paste "Joe Must Go" posters on Boston's subway walls. Pretty soon he met a tiny music major named Jacintha Braga, who was from New Bedford. "For a short time I had two girlfriends," Johnny said.

Johnny was also infatuated with Moira Shearer, the gorgeous sylph of the movie, *The Red Shoes*. But as soon as *A Streetcar Named Desire* buzzed into town, Moira caught competition from an older woman who Johnny thought could only grow more beautiful: Vivian Leigh.

Here's the story, from Johnny's point of view.

I cheated as many hours as I dared off the fifteen I was supposed to log each week working in the dorm cafeteria, which was a condition of my scholarship. Every so often my coach, Doug Raymond, would take me aside for a little shape-up talk. I never warmed to Doug's ex-Navy lieutenant's jargon.

But, running was my youthful passion, and I had been lionized—er, rabbitized—on campus already. Doug had seen to that. A Boston University student newspaper sportswriter had interviewed me right off, and I became known as "Jackrabbit" Kelley.

It was hokey, but for a kid from a small town, suddenly famous in a city college where the enrollment practically equaled my hometown's population, well, it was heady stuff. "The new Gil Dodds," Doug called me in subsequent newspaper interviews, as he prepped me to be a miler on a par with Dodds, who was America's mile champion at the time.

Down the way, off Mass Avenue, holed up in a corner of the ancient Boston Arena, Jock Semple massaged his businessmen and hectored his athletes. Jock, gruff as always, kept open house for his club runners, his BAA boys and, in fact, any runner tough enough to stand his scathing denunciations of everybody and everything that didn't come up to his stringent Scottish standards.

Jock's place quickly became my Saturday morning home. "No posting anti-McCarthy posters today, Paul," I'd tell my pal. "I'm off around Jamaica Pond with Jock's boys."

Jamaica Pond meant twenty miles from the arena through the Fens' serpentine byways, along tree-lined arteries with bumper-to-bumper cars whizzing past, until we reached the mile-and-a-half dirt circuit of the pond in fashionable West Roxbury. I loved the site of Mayor James Michael Curley's fabled brick mansion with its shamrock-carved shutters. Then there was the return run back to the arena. I loved it all!

Jamaica Pond provided a slice of almost suburban countryside in the new and confusing pie of my city life. It was a life hedged by financial and emotional insecurity, and I needed many points of reassuring contact. In the fall of 1950, I depended on Joanie, Jacintha, my widowed mother in New London, my maiden aunt in Norwich, and Jock Semple for emotional reassurance.

Yet Doug Raymond held the key, the scholarship, that is, to my college door. He made no secret of his antipathy toward Jock's "pavement pounders," who would, he hammered, "destroy your natural speed with all that slow distance." But, there was too much happening in the collegiate track world for Doug to dwell on the perils of pavement pounding for more than a few minutes each day.

A Wisconsin kid named Don Gehrman was knocking down 1,000-yard records in the Midwest, and the word was that he'd be making an eastern swing soon. And, a twenty-nine-year-old FBI agent named Fred Wilt was staving off the college kids in the two-mile. Doug liked to think I might come up with "the luck of the Irish" if only he could use his "jackrabbit" to lure Wilt out to BU's Nickerson Field outdoor track.

Wilt had seen the new day, bringing back with him from a trip to Europe the European concept of distance running. He also brought the Swedish word for it: *Fartlek*. Speed play. *Fartlek* was long, untimed runs through scenic countryside instead of a series of hamstring-tightening, stop-watch timed track 440's, staggered by intervals of stand-still rest, which was the system beloved of United States college mentors.

Although the concept of *fartlek* had been developed by the Swedes, for many years the Finns had used the technique, which involved making fast spurts at different points during a run. There was no system to a *fartlek* workout, and those early runners spurted simply for fun, just to break the monotony of a long run.

"How about it Doug?" I coaxed. "What do you think of *fartlek*?"

"Don't you think for a minute, Jackrabbit old boy, that Wilt has forgotten the training that enabled him to get invited to Europe in the first place," Raymond said. "If it weren't for those years of quarter-mile repeats, he wouldn't know *fartlek* from my grandmother's pickle jar."

So much for *fartlek* at BU.

"What do you think, Jock?" I asked.

"Oh, he's onto somethin', all right. It's a far more natural way to train than all that in-an'-out quarter stuff. But we knew it, the idea of it, in the Old Country when I was a young man."

In the end I won some and lost some. I grooved on *The Old Man and the Sea*, and continued to dig poets A. E. Housman and Edwin Arlington Robinson. I worked in the Myles Standish and the BU Commons when I had to, to keep my scholarship. I ran whenever I could—even to Joanie and my mother in Connecticut, and back to Jacintha in Boston. I finagled as many literary courses as the new-fangled computer selection system would let me, and skipped the despised education courses.

When the academic going got tough, I got going, but in the other direction. I dropped two or three required courses, and it started to look like a five-year program for this Johnny Kelley.

Unfortunately, the Korean War precluded five-year under-graduate programs. Even four were hard to hang. I squeaked by the college qualification test to ensure four. But, looking ahead, I could see the dread olive drab uniform.

The bombardment of news came daily from places like Seoul, Inchon, and Pyong-yang. Who could ignore the truth that people, mostly my age, were getting mutilated and killed over there?

General Douglas MacArthur's famous "Old Soldiers Never Die" farewell address to congress was broadcast on the afternoon of April 19, 1951. I heard most of it in static blasts from thousands of hand-carried portable radios in the crowd that lined Exeter Street for the finish of the Boston Marathon that year.

Minutes later, listeners turned their eyes on Japanese runner Shigeki Tanaka, sixth in a line of eleven foreign winners that spanned the years of 1946 through 1956.

That day, although I lost my wallet to a pickpocket, I was determined to race in the Boston Marathon as soon as I could arrange it. When I did, two years later, I had Emil Zatopek to thank. In the 1940s, after the war, Zatopek emerged as the world's leading runner, and much of what we know about the roads today comes from the lessons he taught us.

Zatopek, a burly Czechoslovakian, was a tireless student of running and the body. In the 1948 Olympics he won the 5,000-meter run, and finished just shy of a win in the 10,000-meter. Within the next two years, however, he was breaking world records at every distance, including the marathon.

Zatopek, the Czechoslovakian Choo-Choo, the unbelievable 145-pound human piston, the thrashing, churning, agonizing, grimacing, running automaton, triple gold medalist of the 1952 Helsinki Olympic Games. He was the winner of "the five, the dime, and the Big One." Zatopek achieved his great breakthrough by combining speed work on the track with workouts on the road. If *fartlek* had cracked the door, Zatopek's training regimen broke the fortress.

"I run until I can't run anymore. And then I run some more," Zatopek crowed. And you could see the little boy's love for a game he had learned to play better than any other little boy in the world.

Zatopek's love for running embraced track and forest alike. To Doug Raymond's delight, and Doug lost no opportunity to emphasize his vindication in my eyes, Zatopek thrived on fast 400-meter track intervals, 62 to 68 seconds. Yet the Choo-Choo chugged happily over thirty or forty miles of countryside a day as well.

"He's changed marathon trainin' forever," Jock pronounced. And there wasn't anybody who knew about Zatopek who would have challenged Jock's pronouncement.

Zatopek had become international property, a genuine hero in unheroic terms. Everyone wanted to run like Emil the Great. He lived under a repressive communist regime, yet had forged his own destiny. If you tore a page from Zatopek's book you had to succeed, I believed.

Zatopek married the Czechoslovakian women's Olympic javelin gold medalist. When he couldn't find a log of desired size, he used to run the last hundred meters of his workout carrying his wife, Dana, on his shoulder, or so the legend went.

My own racing, following a modified version of Zatopek's training principles, improved considerably, although I never felt comfortable on the track, especially Doug's indoor boards, and never reached the mile proficiency Doug had prophesied for me. And Doug never hid his disappointment.

"Marathon running changed in the 1940s, which we look at as the start of the modern era," said Jock. "We old plodders began slowing down, but America had never led the world in the marathon anyway. Evolution had always occurred in Europe, and so it did again in the 1940s."

The Finns had long dominated the game. Unlike New England marathoners, they ran throughout the entire year. Runners in Jock's part of the world knocked it off in the winter, and with the cold weather many traveled south to look for work. Runners of Jock's era also believed that a man could burn himself out by running twelve months a year, so they stopped in November and didn't begin training again until February. In Finland, however, runners switched to cross-country skiing once the snow flew.

"We were a different breed, but I can't imagine myself, or DeMar, or Bill Kennedy, or any of us ever skiing," said Jock. "Somehow skiing seemed frivolous, too much like recreation."

While Jock's runners did not train during winter months,

Jock took his United Shoe boys out to Nahant, a stretch of narrow beach north of Boston, on Sundays and walked them through the cold, shallow surf to toughen their feet. Of course, passers-by scorned them, but Jock was never bothered by any of that.

A man endlessly concerned with experimenting, Zatopek tried everything and anything in an effort to make himself stronger and faster. But if it didn't work he'd throw the idea out. Many stories have been circulated about his outlandish practices, but a good number of them are balderdash. For example, I doubt Zatopek ran with a telephone pole strapped to his back, but he pushed himself to the limits in other ways.

Zatopek lived under a Communist regime, and his life, other than running, was strictly regulated by the state. At night, when he found time to run, he marked the distance between street-lamps and ran between them, striding the distance between one, jogging the length of the other. Then he'd stride the next street-lamp, and so on. By incorporating regular spurts, he created the interval workout system.

But Zatopek didn't stop there: to make a workout as intense as possible, he held his breath between streetlamps. Modern runners still employ the interval technique. In fact, Billy Squires, who ran for Jock on the BAA, took Zatopek's ideas a step further in the 1970s. Squires, who coached the Greater Boston track club, put his runners, including Bill Rodgers, through interval miles on the track at Boston College. Before the 1970s, runners rarely did more than quarter-mile intervals on the track, but by extending the distance to a mile, Squires found that his Greater Boston boys could sustain higher speeds in the latter stages of longer races, such as the marathon.

◆

The romantic quality of creating one's own running regime appealed greatly to Jock's young BAA runners in the early 1950s, particularly Johnny Kelley.

Johnny, Jimmy Green, and Al Confalone (the trio that in 1959 took first, second, and fourth at the Pan American Games in Chicago) did not look like rebels. They wore crew cuts and white bucks and the wide-lapel jackets of the period. Nevertheless, in their own way each was seething inside.

As Johnny said, "I've always been awed by Bill Rodgers. I admire the way he acts as a spokesman for change. We never would have done that, get up on a platform and speak out against injustices. We never would have spoken out against the exploitation of runners. But we believed it. I would liken ourselves in the 1950s to the pamphleteers for change, the ones who write slogans on the subway walls. Bill's coming on the scene, compares to the emergence of the Village Voice."

"Don't get me wrong," said Jock. "I didn't encourage the boys to cause problems. In fact, I discouraged them if they spoke out. Johnny had a scholarship to think about and I didn't want him jeopardizing that by antagonizing anyone in authority. That's just the way I am. I don't believe in rebellion. I cared only about making my BAA boys better runners, and better men—and that meant family men. I never cared for politics. So much for my own soapbox. But if the comparison with *fartlek* can be applied, occasionally I'm compelled to put on a spurt of my own."

Just as running was changing in Europe after the war, it was changing in America too, especially on college campuses. Zatopek and others of his generation began to press for workouts that allowed them to express their own individuality. These were kids who took the stories of Zatopek's revolutionary training methods to heart, and suddenly they began to express a desire to experiment.

Most of the kids ran into a brick wall of resistance, however: their college coaches.

"It's important to understand the times," said Jock. "Road running was still considered something the lower class guy did, meaning us plodders, and proper college runners never dropped to that level. In college circles, the mile run was the glamour event, and all the collegians with talent, including Johnny Kelley, were groomed for that."

The accepted workout included only anaerobic running, meaning training that developed a man's middle-distance speed to the greatest pitch. Taking his lead from Zatopek, Johnny began mixing anaerobic speed running with long-slow aerobic running on the roads. Yet all he had to do was mention the word "road," and his Boston University coach, Doug Raymond, hit the roof, because Raymond knew what "road" meant.

It meant Jock.

So during the early going Jock trained his star on the sly.

## Chapter Eleven

### "I was tagged as 'America's Only Hope.'"
### –Johnny Kelley

Jock couldn't hide his pleasure when Johnny announced that he would train for the '53 Boston, but Jock's pole star Scottish pragmatism prompted his admonition. "Look, don't mess yerself up wi' Raymond, boy. Y'need that scholarship. On the other hand, if y'-play yer cards right . . ." Jock's blue eyes twinkled mischievously.

One day at the clinic Jock asked Johnny how Raymond was treating him.

"As usual, Jock. The daily dozen quarters."

"I knew the answer even before I asked," Jock said. "Climb up on my table. Let me show you."

Jock's hand traced a painful path along a muscle in Johnny's upper leg.

"Ouch!"

"That's just to show I know," Jock said. "That hamstring is pretty tight."

Years later, Johnny said, "It was proof that I had experienced before at the master's hands. The man was physiotherapy's answer to Sherlock Holmes."

Of course Jock knew all about Doug Raymond's training methods—well grounded in conventional wisdom as they were. But in the spirit of Boston's post-World War II sports fellowship, it was better not to criticize. If there was criticism to be made, Jock wanted Johnny to initiate it.

Also, despite the mile-deep chasm that separated their training philosophies, Jock and Raymond shared Scottish ancestry and wartime Navy backgrounds. Best not to ripple those waters.

"You can turn over now," Jock said to Johnny. Working on the young man's hamstring, Jock poured warm oil over his calves. Firm hands trundled the flesh.

Resting his head on folded arms, Johnny surveyed Jock's wall, which was covered with a vertical sea of glossy photos: Jock standing beside Boston Garden President Walter Brown, George Mikan on the court ("Best to you, Jock . . . George"), Sonja Henie on ice, Buster Crabbe climbing out of the water, Joe Louis in the squared circle, dancing. It was an impressive photo gallery in the mind of a twenty-year-old Boston University sophomore from New London.

"When Raymond is finished with you, we'll get you into a BAA unicorn jersey for keeps," Jock said.

"So that's what you're keeping me alive for."

"For the most part."

Such was their Saturday morning rubdown ritual, though Johnny's visits were much more than routine. His hamstrings came out hurting after a week of pounding around Doug Raymond's hand-me-down board track at BU.

After the rubdown, it was off to the roads around Jamaica Pond with the BAA gang that had gathered by nine o'clock. For complaining stragglers, Jock fired a stock shot. "You think nine is early. When I worked as a ship fitter, I sometimes had to run in pitch dark at four o'clock in the morning."

No matter what time Johnny arrived at the old Saint Botolph Street arena, he'd find Jock bustling around his small side room.

More than once, Johnny suspected Jock had spent the night sleeping on his massage table. Someday, Jock's runners joked, we'll show up and find no arena, just Jock Semple working unperturbed amid the rubble. A year later the joke nearly came true with the arena's destruction by fire.

After George Younis, a member of their road running group, arrived from Dorchester one Saturday toting his running gear wrapped in a towel, Johnny and the others moved out to make room for Jock's paying customers. "I love my patients, but they don't want to exercise," Jock once said. "They just want to feel like they've exercised."

"Who else have you found at school that might join the club?" he asked Johnny later.

As Johnny explained it, "I told Jock about my new friend, George Leslie. But Leslie, a Cambridge commuter, had already been approached by Fred Brown for his North Medford Club. I broached that development diplomatically, then hurried into my running gear to get out of point-blank range. Brown's very name often incited Jock to explosive fury.

"Now, what's Fred Brown got to offer a youngster?" Jock said. "His club is falling apart. They don't even have a clubhouse. In fact, there's no such place as North Medford."

"Oh, they've had some good ones, Jock," Younis countered. "What about Crane and Mederos?"

"What are Crane and Mederos doing these days? George, all the good young runners are comin' to us. In a year, Fred Brown will have nothin' but a bunch of ham an' eggers!"

"How's that Jock? Ham an' eggers?" Another voice joined the chorus. It belonged to Quincyite Don Fay, a member of the running group whose MO was a persistent, gentle questioning of Jock's colorful words.

"You know what a ham an' egger is, Don. It's a poor son-of-a-gun that joins the North Medford Club instead of the BAA."

At that point three more runners turned up, ready to go, and I thanked Jock for the rubdown, for making my legs feel like new springs again.

"Well, just don't go doin' any more quarters until Raymond points a loaded gun at you," Jock said. "What you need today is a nice, easy twenty miles wi' our BAA boys here, out around the reservoir.

"I'll see you next week," I promised.

"Remember to try to talk Raymond into lettin' you do some slow distance, in place of those everlastin' quarters. Also, keep Leslie away from Brown and North Medford."

◆

During this time, Johnny worked as a short-order cook at night at the old 1326 Hayes-Bickford on Mass Avenue in Harvard Square. Saturdays, he worked in the basement of a jewelry store lugging boxes.

"I have to say one thing about Johnny," said Jock many years later. "He only looked like an easy touch. He's sweet, but that's a steel rod he carried around for a spinal cord. I knew that about Johnny, that he was going to do workouts he created himself. I never claimed to be Johnny's coach. A father figure to him, yes. And that was coach enough."

More from Johnny:

One Monday, after my last class, I loped down to the improvised BU track locker room in Bay State Road's School of Education basement.

As I was tying my second shoe, Doug Raymond whistled in, stop watch in hand. "Well, Jackrabbit," he chortled. "We've got a humdinger of a workout lined up for today."

"Not—"

"You got it. We're going to bang out a dozen quarters between 60 and 65 seconds."

"You know, Doug," I dared. "Jock thinks I could use a bit of slow distance sometimes during the week."

"Gosh darn it all! Who asked Jock?" Raymond turned as volcanic as his Scottish counterpart. "You're a collegian, not a darn club runner. If those people could run, they'd be in college, not shuffling around Jamaica Pond. Now listen to me, stick with my program, or you'll become just another club-running ham and egger."

"Ham and egger?"

"Yes. A ham and egger is a poor son-of-a-gun who passes up college and loses all his speed jogging with a darn fool bunch of road runners. Do you suppose any one of those so-called athletes would run a marathon if he could run a four-minute mile? Of course not. They're all old men, way past an age when they have any right to compete. They're unable to play a skill sport, so they take to plodding through that annual parade.

"Now, what do you want, Johnny? A young man's deserved glory, or a few days' headlines for trying to outrun a bunch of has-beens and never was ham and eggers? Don't bother me with this nonsense again, I don't want to hear that word 'road' again."

Johnny, of course, went right ahead and mixed Doug Raymond's kind of work with the Zatopek style of training. Finally, he got Doug Raymond to compromise: Johnny agreed to work out at Boston University with the team, but Doug had to allow him to incorporate Zatopek's continuous running with his speed work.

On Sundays Johnny ran twelve to fifteen miles along the Charles River. Right there you can see the difference between training then and training now. In 1953, while training seriously for his first marathon, Johnny did but fifteen miles for a long Sunday run. Today the top runners don't look at anything less than twenty. Today they run 130 to 150 miles a week. Right there, you can see one reason why marathon times have come down.

Johnny took Mondays off. On Tuesdays he worked out at Boston University. While the rest of the team ran quarter-mile sprints on the board track, Johnny worked Raymond for permission to run around Braves Stadium, which circled the track.

He pushed himself to his physical limits with the same zeal employed by Zatopek—short of the telephone pole, that is. Johnny tapered off on Wednesdays, running four to six miles on the track. On Thursdays he came back up again, running as hard as he did on Tuesdays. Once in a while, though, Raymond collared him and made him run with the team. Jock would get him afterward, when he'd come in with calves as tight as bowstrings.

On Fridays, Johnny eased up, then ran a meet on Saturdays, or came by Jock's clinic for long slow distance with the BAA boys.

One method remained for putting additional miles on his legs: in the evening after classes and his workout, Johnny took another run from Back Bay to his job at Hayes-Bickford.

"My God, Johnny!" Jock exclaimed one time. "When do ya take a shower? D'ya just climb into your apron?"

Johnny smiled the famous Kelley smile. "Jock, in the short order cook business, nobody notices."

◆

Training for the 1953 Boston Marathon meant balancing a crazy load of bric-a-brac, perpetually about to topple. Two weeks after Johnny prevailed on Doug Raymond to let him try the '53 Boston (he had kept the news from him as long as possible) Johnny administered the coup de grace: he told Doug, through his friend, George Terry, that he was going to marry Jacintha Braga, the petite music major he had been dating.

"Jeepers Crow, I can't believe it," came Doug's reply, via George.

"What else did he say?" Johnny asked.

"That was it, lad. Not exactly 'many happy returns.'"

The third floor room with kitchenette (hotplate, no refrigerator) at 477 Beacon Street overlooked one of Back Bay's eternal garbage can alleys. Sooty windows filtered sunlight to the strength of a Dracula moon. Nevertheless, the place became home for Johnny and Jessie late on the night of January 17, a night when he also ran anchor on a two-mile relay in Boston Garden at the Knights of Columbus track meet.

"Is this kid of yours nuts?" Johnny's new father-in-law, Tony Braga, piped that morning at eleven as the couple married in New Bedford.

"Oh, Daddy," Jessie said, "he just likes to run."

Mr. Braga was not assuaged. Nor was he alone in his incredulity. "Jesus, Kelley, you got ashes for brains? By the time you get home you'll only be good in bed for sleep," rang the chorus from his teammates.

With two laps to go in the race, the band struck up "Here Comes the Bride." Somehow the word had got around, and Johnny glanced around to catch the culprit. Jock smiled as he flashed the lap cards. Smiling his own smile, Johnny brought the team home in first.

Not too long after that, winter began to lose its grip, and Johnny's enthusiasm for the marathon race rose with the sap in the trees along Commonwealth Avenue. He and Jessie managed to scrape up sixty-four dollars a month to pay the rent, while keeping their perishables chilled on the window ledge. With the coming of spring, Johnny joined the BAA boys more often.

The road racing season began as the indoor season finished at BU, and finally Doug conceded Johnny's right to run twenty-six miles. "Okay, Okay," he consented. "But you wear one of our BU jerseys, understand? I don't want to see your picture in the paper in a unicorn."

Johnny won the time prize at the Hyde Shoe race, a twelve-mile handicap run through Cambridge in March. A week later, he won again at the Cathedral ten-mile, but this time victory came the hard way. Browning Ross, the "flying letter carrier" from Philadelphia (as he was called in tribute to his day job as a mail-man), gave Johnny a go right from the gun. Johnny inched away over Telegraph Hill's cobblestones five miles out, and ran as if the Devil himself pursued him over the rest of the windswept South Boston course, to edge Ross by ten seconds.

"My God, Jock, Ross is thirty-three years old, and primarily an indoor runner," Johnny marveled as he submitted to Jock's muscle relaxing ministrations after the race.

"Ooh, yeah, he's no spring chicken like yourself," Jock admitted. "But, on the other hand, he's just turned to road racin'. His legs haven't found out what all that poundin' can do to 'em yet." He winked as he baby-oiled Johnny's sore calves.

Ross had entered the Boston Marathon too, but Johnny didn't fear him at that distance. He'd be tough up to fifteen miles, he knew. After that, his on-the-toes style—suitable to middle-distance running—would do him in over the longer haul.

Johnny's wife started a wall chart of his daily training. She called it the Jessie Kelley-O-Graph. By the first of April, it showed six weeks in a row where Johnny had run more than sixty-five miles. His greatest week's mileage was eighty-five. His average: seventy-two.

Then two weeks before the race, American aspirants got the bad news. Japanese and Finnish teams were coming. The Finns, in fact, had already quartered themselves at their American-Finnish home away from home in Danielson, Connecticut, guzzling buttermilk and (according to their host) "plenty of coffee" and training twice a day.

Johnny was tagged as "America's Only Hope," a name he was to wear every April for the next ten years. "It did imply a certain urgency to 'bring home the bacon,' or some such thing," said Johnny. "There I'd be, serving up a dish of Hayes-Bickford beans and a photographer would pop a camera over the counter. 'What's happening?' a mystified customer would exclaim. 'Haven't ya heard?' Pete, our voluble, drunken cook yelled from the stove: 'Johnny here's America's Only Hope.'"

Luckily for his strained relationship with Doug Raymond, one pre-race picture was shot at Braves Field and included the caption: COACH AND PROTÉGÉ ON EVE OF THE BIG RACE—BU STAR IS AMERICA'S ONLY HOPE.

Johnny hoped Doug wouldn't blow up. "I wouldn't miss the Boston Marathon for the world," Doug was quoted in one paper, and Johnny shuddered to think that Doug and Jock might both meet him at the finish line.

Back at his clinic, Jock boiled. "Raymond's suddenly discovered his long-lost love for the marathon. He better brush up on Japanese."

"Japanese?"

"No offense. You're gain' to do okay, but, Johnny, I watched those Japanese practicin' out on the course today, an' jeez, nobody's gain' to beat them."

"What about me, Jock?"

"Ooh, let's see. It's your first marathon unless we count the '49 race when y'didn't finish. Still, you're in great shape. But there are the Finns, too. So, I'd pick you for about fifth."

For Johnny, waiting for Boston was like waiting for Christmas. When the day dawned cloudy and cool, with a brisk northwest wind, it was just right for a record.

"By Framingham I had proved to myself that I could run at least partway with the best of the foreigners," Johnny later said. "Austin Scott of New York, the Finns, the Japanese, and I remained bunched at the top after seven miles. I knew our pace was fast, but I held on.

"From miles six to ten I ran stride for stride with a tiny Japanese robot whose name I didn't know. I knew only that he was a full head shorter than I and his eyes bore relentlessly ahead. Whenever a strip of grass appeared, he leapt onto it to break the shock of the pavement."

Scott tired and fell back outside Natick at ten miles, but Johnny hung onto his Japanese sidekick. They resembled two wind-swept leaves as they tore through Natick soundlessly, faster than Johnny had planned, faster than he had believed himself capable of running over such a long stretch. Faster, in fact, than he was capable of running much farther.

"By Wellesley I had spent the best of my juice, and I watched helplessly as the tiny Japanese fellow picked up the pace; as if borne by a slightly greater breeze, he moved yard by yard out ahead of me," Johnny said. "I ran now in second place, but soon I was passed by the Finn, Veikko Karvonen, whom we had overtaken in Natick.

Then a second Japanese overtook me, followed by Karl Leanders-
son of Sweden.

"I tried to shut out both the spectators' voices and thoughts
of the distance remaining as I slogged over Newton's hills. At Lake
Street, twenty-one miles, I walked briefly, only to find that my
strength had returned. Before anyone else could overhaul me, I gut-
ted it out down Beacon Street, through Kenmore Square past my
own neighborhood, then, miraculously, Commonwealth Avenue.
Then Exeter Street arrived. I kicked past the Exeter Theatre (Alec
Guinness in *Kind Hearts and Coronets*), sprinted with the welcoming
cheers of the crowd ringing in my ears, and, lunging, crossed the
pot-hole finish line in front of the door of the Lenox Hotel."

Then it was over. Jock wrapped Johnny in a scratchy but oh
so warm army blanket, and together they stumbled through the
parting crowd toward the door of the Soden Building. "My God,
Johnny, you ran great! Just like I said! To the very place!"

"I was fifth?"

"Yes, fifth!" Jock shouted. "An' first American!"

"Jock," I struggled to form the question, "who . . . who?"

"Yamada. Keizo Yamada. Y'never saw anybody so tiny."

"Oh yes, I did," I said, too exhausted to elaborate. "I saw."

"He looked like a wind would blow 'im away," Jock continued. "But, cripes! He busted the old record all t'hell, Johnny. Yamada ran 2:18:51."

Jock and Johnny were among the first into the Soden Building's basement where cots awaited spent bodies. Jock fell to unlac-
ing his flats, and a hand clapped his shoulder.

"Jackrabbit, you came through!" Doug Raymond exulted.

Johnny smiled weakly while Jock grumbled at his laces.

"For gosh sakes, you really were America's Only Hope,"
Doug said.

More audible grumbling. Suddenly Raymond noticed his BAA counterpart.

"What d'ya think of him, Jock? Wasn't he great? Wouldn't you say his performance is worth my talking to the athletic director at BU about our getting him a special jersey for the race next year?"

"Yeah. One wi' a unicorn on it," Jock shot back without looking up.

Johnny knew right then that there could be no ducking the difficult choice ahead.

## Chapter Twelve

## "The truth was that I never discriminated against anyone for race, creed, or color, only for being slow."
### –Jock Semple

"Oh, the loonies! Today we get guys who wear cow-heads in the Boston Marathon. We get comedians who come in space suit costumes and superman togs. But that was still years away in 1954 when Boston featured the Race of Champions," said Jock.

That year a much-publicized duel developed in the press between Olympic champion Delfo Cabrera and Britain's Jim Peters. Veikko Karvonen and Erkki Puolakka of Finland, and the Japanese champion, Karau Horoshima, were also listed at the top. But that Peters, the world-record holder, had decided to come to Boston was big news, and it was Jock who brought him.

For years Jock had been watching Peters. He was an Englishman and Jock was proud of the new ground he was breaking in the marathon. Only nine marathons had been run in less than 2:20, and Peters owned three of them. In the Windsor Castle to Chiswick race he broke the world record with a 2:18:40. His time was so much better than anyone in England had ever run before, so the officials measured the course—and found that it was 370 yards too long!

Early in 1954 Jock received a letter from Peters expressing a desire to run Boston, but he had no money for expenses.

"The Boston Marathon committee never has and never will, so long as I have breath to holler, extended expense money to any runner," said Jock. "Still, I was delighted, and so in lieu of support from the British Amateur Athletic Board, I began a fundraising campaign on my own to bring Jim Peters to Boston."

Jock received help from the press, especially Jerry Nason, Gerry Hern, and Dave Egan, who publicized the campaign, but still the going was slow. Yet the date for the marathon was drawing near, and Jock wrote to Jim to guarantee expenses for him, even if he had to pay it all himself.

"Well, you know Murphy's Law," said Jock. "By the time Peters landed at Logan Airport, I had put up three hundred dollars out of my own pocket. That worked out to income from working thirty basketball games at the Garden. But I did manage to secure a promise from a TV station. Executives there promised to interview Jim after the race and payment from that would defray the costs I had absorbed.

"I don't regret spending the money. We meet so few gentlemen in life that I'd pay all over again for the chance to help Jim Peters."

◆

With the Boston papers hyping the Race of Champions, Johnny Kelley just couldn't wait for April 19. Doug grudgingly conceded to yet another Boston, "but only Boston, mind you" Marathon. Their precarious partnership now seemed pegged on the long, long shot of Johnny winning the thing. He took a trial spin over the course a short month before the event, and, looking back, he could hardly believe his time of 2:28 plus. In practice, to boot.

Johnny jogged home after his last class. He stayed long enough to stoke up on a peanut butter sandwich and tell Jacintha they were going to meet Doug and his assistant, Ed Flanagan, at Kenmore Square, and then drive to Hopkinton for the start of the marathon.

Johnny placed seventh that day in 1954, still first American, with a time a few seconds slower than he had put up in 1953. He crossed the finish line wearing Jock's BAA unicorn jersey for the first time. Although his final break with Doug was still a month away, he had performed a symbolic liberation by choosing to wear the unicorn emblem. In every marathon thereafter, he ran unencumbered by his difficult dual loyalty.

"Curiously enough, Jock didn't catch me up in his army blanket at the finish of my 1954 Boston Marathon," Johnny said. "A few minutes earlier he had caught British champion Jim Peters, the world record-holder and generally regarded to be the world's best. Only Jim hadn't won the 1954 Boston Marathon. He had finished an exhausted second.

"Years later, poring through a shoe box of photographs, I spotted a shot of Peters on his cot minutes after Jock had deposited him there," said Johnny. "Peters looked like a man who had swum away from the wreck of the Hesperus in his skivvies. Smiling, he propped himself on a matchstick right arm, raising his left to signal thumbs-up."

"Peters finished a disappointing and disappointed second to Finland's champion, Veikko Karvonen, in Boston's Race of Champions," Johnny continued. "It certainly had been a race to remember. But nobody would have blamed Peters for trying to blot it out. The man had good reason to wish the whole preceding week undone. Nevertheless, Jim Peters, game Briton, world's hardest working champion and all-around good sport, smiled for the camera. And why not? Wasn't Jim Peters entitled to an off day?"

When you consider his preceding week, you have no trouble thinking he was not his best. After much bureaucratic haggling over the terms of Peters' trip, the British Board finally consented to let him travel to America. On April 15, four days before the race, the runner's flight took off from London. What happened next might have given Peters a hint of things to follow. Engine trouble forced a landing in Edinburgh. After several hours' delay, Peters and his Board assigned "nanny," Jack Crump, were again airborne, en route to Boston, where Jock Semple awaited their scheduled six P.M. arrival.

Around six-thirty, Logan Airport officials informed Jock that Peters' plane was circling fog-shrouded Boston, unable to land. The flight would likely go on to Washington, to National Airport. Jock ground his teeth and steeled himself for the four-hundred-mile drive.

Then, within moments, the pilot received clearance to land. Five minutes later, Jock Semple embraced a boy from home. Then they headed for Back Bay's smack on the finish line Hotel Lenox and a night of deserved, already delayed, rest.

"Say Jock, is that Jim Peters with you?" the lobby lounger who looked suspiciously like a sports reporter called out as Jock squired the champion and his nanny to the Lenox registration desk.

"Maybe it is, and maybe it isn't, but I wouldn't tell you, either way," Jock replied with a rare effort at tact. "The fact is, this man has just flown the Atlantic and he needs a good night of undisturbed sleep."

So Jim Peters might have taken his rightful rest. Only, being Jim Peters, he undid himself: "Oh, I say, Jock, I can spare a few minutes." Three hours later, the reporter had his interview and Peters had the feeling of having been up a long time.

Peters arose the next day after four hours' sleep. Through the Lenox's revolving door, he loped smack into the teeth of a Boston nor'easter. He quickly revolved back upstairs to the telephone.

Jock didn't have to twist Jim's leg to convince him to run his planned ten miles round and round the middle tier of Boston Garden's gallery. One hundred laps around the cement catwalk re-inflated the blisters Peters had incurred in a club race the previous weekend. Jock opened and poulticed them. Still, his prize import left Jock's salon hobbling.

If you don't like New England weather, wait ten minutes. Peters waited a day. Frigid rain gave way to near tropical soup. Jock drove Peters out to Hopkinton for a six-mile tune-up over the marathon's opening miles. Two miles out, Peters limped alongside his host's car complaining of stiffness in his right thigh. He finished his tour in the car, then repaired to Jock's parlor for the master's tenderizing massage. It proved so revitalizing that he decided to knock off a repeat ten-mile go in the Garden.

The day before the race brought no further problems, and events seemed to be taking a turn for the better when race day dawned cloudy and cool, London-style.

Jock was ebullient. "Jim, I got a call from a local businessmen's club last night. They want to honor you at their monthly dinner tonight . . . after your victory." He dropped his voice confidentially, "And they're goin' t'hand you a check."

On the line, eight national marathon champions of their respective countries glittered among two hundred starters. Ceremonially, Argentina's Dolfo Cabrera, 1948 Olympic Marathon winner, had received the lion's share of pre-race attention. But, at thirty-seven, out of top condition, he didn't have a reasonable chance. Smart money rode on either Peters, or his nemesis, Finland's Karvonen.

Karvonen made no secret of his desire to revenge himself on Peters, as Jim had humiliated him with a seven-minute victory in a marathon at Turku, Finland the previous summer. From the gun, the unsmiling, thin-thatched blond Finn ran as if alone. Peters contented himself to hang with the pack of frontrunners a few strides off Karvonen's pace, until six miles. Then he said, "This is where the fun begins," and he moved on the Finn.

Jim Peters' fun lasted until the pair crested Heartbreak Hill. There, Karvonen accelerated briefly. It was an inconsequential maneuver to the uninitiated spectator, but it was fraught with significance for the press bus sharpies. And for Jim. That little spurt foretold the race's end. After twenty-one miles of even-money dueling, Karvonen's legs were still tensile springs; Peters' legs had turned to rubber.

Karvonen allowed the merest hint of a smile to light his stolid face as he breasted the tape. Two minutes later, a grim, gone, but still game Jim Peters collapsed into Jock's arms and blanket.

"Look out! Get aside!" the chagrined Scot bellowed to the curbside crowd.

Then two bodies hit the cement together, one wrapped in a blanket, the other topped off with a chapeau.

"Jeez!" Jock exclaimed.

"Oof!" Jim gasped.

It was as if an ambulance carrying a dying man had crashed on its way to the hospital. Downstairs, doctors rushed to Jim Peters' cot. They found only a bruised elbow on top of a case of acute depletion. Their patient would live to do it again.

Jock, meanwhile, had been taken to answer a phone call. When he came back to Jim's side, he was bristling mad. "Those so and so's! They heard you finished second, and they cancelled your invitation," he told the limp body.

"Oh, that's all right," Jim smiled up. "I wouldn't have had time to shop for gifts for my family tonight if I'd had to star at their banquet."

Then he gave the old thumbs up, and Jock smiled too, watching in his mind's eye the three hundred dollars the TV station had promised him as reimbursement for Peter's expenses take wings and fly away!

◆

The Peters affair may be the most famous of Jock's international incidents, but he dealt with the world every year. Often the encounter was a comedy of errors.

JOCK TAKES OVER—KOREANS ARRIVE FOR RRRRRACE
by Tim Horgan
*Boston Herald*
April 14, 1966

Jock Semple's face lit up like dawn on the Firth of Forth and his voice burbled like the Sound of Sleet.

"It's Choi! It's Choi!" Jock yelled and ran out the door and gave a hug and pat on his swarthy cheek to a grinning Oriental. One of the photographers made it 8 to 5 the grinning Oriental would give Jock a shot on the jaw.

This was at the TWA terminal at Logan Airport at the unsightly hour of 8:35 yesterday morning. Jock, the unpaid and completely uninhibited greeter for the Boston Marathon, was out to meet a two-man Korean team, plus coach.

Before the plane got in Jock was hoping the coach would be Choi Yoon Chil.

"He rrrran herrrre yearrrrs ago," said Jock in his remarkable burr. "I know him verrrry well. Of course he speaks English. I taught him myself."

Just the same, Jock had invited a Korean who works at Channel 2 to serve as interpreter, but the man hadn't shown.

"If Choi is the coach, we won't need him," Jock promised, "I'll be the interpreter."

So it turned out to be Choi and Jock said to stand back, he'd do the talking.

"Mr. Choi," Jock said. "This is a Boston sportswriter."

"Yes, yes," said Mr. Choi, grinning to beat the band.

"Do your runners speak English too, Mr. Choi?"

"Yes, yes."

"What's your names, boys?"

One boy stared out the window. The other stared at Jock.

"Don't they speak English?" Jock asked Mr. Choi.

"No," said Mr. Choi.

"Get their names, Jock," said the sportswriter.

Jock did, after a slam-bang battle. Kim Bok Nae and Yoo Nyng Jong.

"Ask him what the boys do in Korea, Jock."

"What-boys-do-in-Korea?" asked Jock.

"Yes," replied Mr. Choi. "Yes."

"No, no," said Jock. "What-boys-do-in-Korea!"

"Students," said Mr. Choi.

"In Seoul?"

"Yes, yes. Choun Chun University."

"They're students at Choun Chun University in Seoul," Jock announced.

"No, in Choun Chun," said Mr. Choi.

"Where the hell's that guy from Channel 2?" asked Jock.

"We take part in Boston Marathon games," Mr. Choi recited.

"No, no," said Jock.

"No?" said Mr. Choi, looking worried.

"I mean, why did you pick these two . . . I give up,"

Jock said. He mopped his brow. Mr. Choi grinned. One of the photographers made it 8 to 5 that Jock would slug Mr. Choi.

"Did you boys ever race against the Japanese, Mr. Choi?"

"Fowst," replied Mr. Choi. "Fowst time Kim."

"We better forget that," warned Jock. "How-many-rrrrraces-have-they-rrrrrun?" asked Jock.

"Rrrrraces!" said Mr. Choi, his face cloudy with thought. "Rrrraces?"

"Rrrrraces!" shouted Jock. "Rrrraces!"

"Ah, yes. Rrrrraces," said Mr. Choi.

"Ah, well," said Jock. "It'll make no difference a hundred years from now."

Another year, another Boston Marathon with Jock at the helm!

# Chapter Thirteen

## "They had sciatica when they came to me, but the cops pinched them in a more painful manner."
### –Jock Semple

JOCK ENTERTAINED THE INFAMOUS as well as the famous at the Garden, and once even had three Brinks security employees come into his clinic for a treatment.

"It was a Sunday and it was slow when a fella rapped at my door and asked if I could take a look at a couple of bad backs," Jock said. "It's hard for me to say no to somebody who waves at me with a picture of Ulysses S. Grant, and I said sure. A moment later in walk three muffins, all shapes and sizes, and I gave them a treatment. The lead man said they'd come by again the next Sunday, and I was counting the dollars, but I didn't see the trio again until I saw their picture in the paper after their arrest for the Brinks robbery job.

Jock had been cultivating most of his runners since they were schoolboys, developing them for the BAA team. As they grew older they got stronger, and the team benefited. Johnny Kelley was the team leader, and Jimmy Green right behind him. Jimmy finished second to Johnny at the Pan Am Games in 1959. At one time,

Jimmy had been a boxer. He was an intense guy, and when he ran he attacked the course.

"Jimmy Green crosses the line at Boston like a man threshing wheat," Jerry Nason once wrote when Jimmy was widely recognized as one of the best road runners in America.

Only a handful of people could beat Jimmy Green in a marathon, and even fewer could beat him for brains. A teacher as well as a world-class runner, he never wanted to be regarded as one-dimensional, so he drove himself to be the best both in his sport and in his intellectual pursuits. Jock always said that Jimmy added class to his shop.

Al Confalone, another of Jock's BAA stars, gave the impression of being relaxed. The youngest boy in a large family, Al lived at home with his mother. His was a real Italian home, and many times his mother fed mountains of pasta to an army of BAA boys after races. Inwardly, Al was as intense as Jimmy or Johnny. At a time when the world-record hovered in the area of 2:20, Al took a 2:42 talent and drove himself to run 2:28.

He'd run to work, sixteen miles away in Salem, running the whole thing hard right down the median strip along Route 128, a major highway. Then he would flip. If getting up at four-thirty in the morning to train didn't produce instant results, Al might let it all go to hell, and fall completely out of shape. Yet he was the gentlest of all the boys.

"Scotto Gonzales/Gonzales Scotto (again they never knew since he signed his name both ways,) Tony Sapienza, and Jerry Harvey rounded out the team. "But I had one imp, Don Fay," Jock said. "Oh, did he torment me! A hard-working businessman as well as runner, for years Don supplied me with sponges. He owned a small company, one of the last to make natural sponges and for years I used Don's free sponges to water down my runners in races.

Nobody was more loyal than Don. We could always depend on him to be the fifth man on our team."

Traveling with those boys was a lot of fun, but the fun was sometimes laced with perilous excitement.

"Once, at Three Rivers, Canada, I was servicin' my boys in the marathon and there was another car staying right beside Gerry Cote," Jock said. "I got in an altercation with the driver when he sideswiped my car which was a month old. We had a little fisticuffs. In short, he came out worse than I fared."

An on-looker called a policeman and Jock explained what had happened. The cop took Jock's registration and said he'd hear from them. Jock waited in some anxiety for a few weeks, but the call never came. Later, a newspaperman embellished the story, giving Jock a broken tooth and saying he spent a week on his rubdown table back at the Garden, afraid to go home.

"Can you believe that?" Jock asked. "One, somebody saying I had a busted tooth. And a second writer said I had two black eyes. I'm just happy Semple can put food on those reporter guys' tables with their nonsense."

◆

One day in 1954, just before the Canadian Marathon Championships, Scotto took a fall. That's what Al Confalone heard from Don Fay anyway. It seemed the friendly, albeit mysterious little man with the slight Spanish accent and the reversible name (sometimes Scotto Gonzales, other times Gonzales Scotto) tumbled from his window-washer's perch and landed in a hedge five stories below. The hedge, and Scotto's tangled harness, likely saved his life.

Johnny Kelley, of course, had his side of the story.

We picked Confalone to tell Jock, who was busy at the Garden making last minute preparations before gathering us all into the car for the long ride to the Canadian Marathon Championship. Fay had nominated Confalone because he was the club's most diplomatic (or fearless) member.

Al reported to Jock while the rest of us huddled behind him in the door to Jock's clinic. Jock had entered our BAA team as his A team in the belief that soon we'd be not only American champions, but North American champions.

"Jock, Scotto took a bad fall today," Al said.

"It wasn't over a girl, I hope," Jock joked, oblivious to calamity as he moved a man from the diathermy to the whirlpool.

Confalone gained strength, surmising that Jock had already voiced his worst fear. "No, not a girl, Jock. A building. He fell five stories."

"Five stories! He'd a' been killed!"

"He was lucky, Jock. He's not dead."

Jock suddenly felt the impact. "Oh, jeez! He may not be able to run the race Monday."

Within an hour the victim himself appeared in Jock's Boston Garden establishment and Jock bent over Scotto's obviously living remains, gently tapping his way south. His patient didn't flinch, but our gallery voiced the pain Scotto must have felt.

"What're you groanin' for?" Jock asked no one in particular among our group.

"That probing must hurt," Jimmy Green said.

"You don't know that. Scotto is the one to say. Does it hurt, Scotto?"

The little man smiled gamely. He could have been a nobleman or a peasant in his former country. We never knew which country that was. "It's kind of sore, in the ribs," he said.

"Well, Scotto, you're a tough man, an' you've survived a bad fall. There's nothin' broken that I can tell. How do you feel about runnin' Monday?"

"Running Monday!" The gallery harmonized its disbelief. "Jock, he just fell five stories."

"Scotto's alive," Jock exclaimed. "Why shouldn't he run?"

"Maybe he suffered a trauma," Green essayed.

"Arrgh, Jimmy! Trauma's for characters in those Russian novels of yours. What about it, Scotto?"

"I'd like to run, Jock," Scotto managed. "Yes. I run."

Half an hour later, everyone piled into the Toronado, as Jock elbowed wide. "No need to squeeze in this luxury boat, boys. Give Scotto's ribs plenty of room," he said.

On the flat road from Granby to St. Hyacinthe where the marathon was contested, our collective concern for Scotto soon gave way to concentration on personal survival in the day's blasting heat. By the time I had finally hauled my sodden BAA unicorn across the line a winner, I was told that the rest of the field had taken a dip in the Yamaska River, which flowed beside the course.

Huge gaps separated the finishers. I didn't know how much, if at all, everyone's swim affected the finishing order. But then it was announced that our BAA team had harvested the gold with Scotto's help. The unbreakable window-washer had nailed fifth among our A team finishers, and clinched the title for us.

During Molson Brewery's party for the runners afterwards, Jock made his way to the table where our A team engaged in some sanctioned elbow-bending.

"You all ran great," Jock crowed. Then, to Scotto, "How do your ribs feel now?"

"You know, they seem better. I think maybe my swim helped them."

"Why, of course it did. A refreshing swim in the midst of a hot marathon is as good as a whirlpool treatment."

As exhausted as we were, the free flowing beer blurred our pain and turned our minds to future successes.

"I can't wait for the cross country this year," Jock said, envisioning a second harvest. "I can tell you this: we're goin' to have a great fall."

Fay looked impish. "Jock, Scotto's already had a great fall!"

Jock made as if to cuff his team's gadfly, but instead, he smiled at Fay, and then signaled to the waitress, allowing him another sanctioned beer.

◆

After that race in 1954, the army got Johnny Kelley for a time. "Trying to pick up where I had left off in Boston after that proved at once easier and more difficult than I had expected," Johnny said. "Easier because the GI Bill gave me the grand amount of $120 a month. In the parlance, I had never had it so good, financially anyway."

Johnny still had to work, and did that in the cellar of Thomas Long's venerable downtown jewelry store. He wasn't sure he liked being a twenty-five-year-old stock boy. But it improved on the short-order cook business, for sure.

Johnny returned to BU full time in 1955 to qualify for full GI payments, though he needed only those two dropped courses and eight weeks of student teaching to come out with a teaching degree.

On the flip side, life after the army was harder for Johnny because the marathon world had taken many an exciting turn. During his absence, Boston had become the marathon world's center.

Adding to his apprehension was his friend Nick Castes' part in the marathon revolution. Applying "Zatopekian principles" of training, he had broken the 2:20 barrier in the 1955 race, to place fifth, first American, in that record-smashing field. Japanese Hideo Hamamura lowered his countryman Yamada's record to another unbelievable figure, 2:18:22.

"Get yer mileage up, inject the right amount of interval work, race every so often, an' come in fer regular massages an' diathermy treatments, an' you'll run wi' the best of 'em, mark my word," Jock reassured Johnny.

Johnny's thoughts were a little different, however.

I followed Jock's prescription. For the mileage, I commenced getting up and out along the Charles River Esplanade each morning at four-thirty. For four months before the 1956 Marathon, I made sixteen miles a morning five days a week.

I saw the city and the river as only a few lone wolves saw it. If ever there was an unarguable break between the old and the new, that break with the old marathon came in the 1956 Boston. The first of two United States Olympic tryouts, Boston drew the best of the new breed of upper distance track runners with marathon aspirations, fellows like Joe Tyler, Fred Wilt, and Gordon McKenzie—all speed runners who were giving the marathon a try.

When it was over, three of us—Nick Costes, and Dean Thackwray and I—had thrust our best feet forward into the doorway to the 1956 Olympics, and the three of us qualified for the US Olympic marathon team. But the big news was the winning time posted by a Finnish Army sergeant named Antti Viskari, an eye-boggling 2:14:14, a Boston Marathon and a world record.

All I knew was that Viskari and I had given it everything, stride for stride for twenty-five miles and then some, on a cool, cloudy day, aided by a brisk northwest breeze, and that when I had to let him go in the last half mile, it wasn't from exhaustion but from inability to run faster that I let him slip away. I was still belting out that final mile, but I finished twenty seconds too late in 2:14:34, while Nick hauled in fourth in 2:18:01, and Dean Thackwray fifth in 2:20:40.

Jock was ecstatic. Dean and I were both BAA boys.

"My God, there's never been anythin' like this!" Jock said. "Walter Brown is going to go crazy with delight!"

We didn't stop smiling until two weeks later when the course was re-measured and found to be some eleven hundred yards short. We had to pick up the pieces and lay 'em down, disappointed as we were to have our world-beating times erased. But, Boston's top three Americans had all made it to Melbourne, where the Olympics were held in the late fall to coincide with the cooler weather in the southern hemisphere, and more disappointment awaited: Nick finished twentieth, I was twenty-first (after leading for a time before wilting in the heat,) and Dean dropped out. Alain Mimoun won the Olympic Marathon and Zatopek, now the old warrior, had come back six weeks after a hernia operation to place fifth.

On December 7, 1956, the team's homebound Olympic DC-6 stopped over a day in Oahu. It was the fifteenth anniversary of Pearl Harbor, and Alain Mimoun had won the Olympic Marathon. Zatopek, now the old warrior, had come back six weeks after a hernia operation to place fifth.

I pondered retirement as our plane winged toward LA. I really beat myself up over my poor showing. I had graduated from Boston University and was now a junior high school reading teacher in Groton, Connecticut. The kids were all playing Elvis when I returned. Like the pace of the modern marathoner, Elvis's music moved faster than anything before it.

By the time I returned home from the Olympics there were two weeks of teaching remaining before the Christmas break. All I knew was that I was ready for that vacation. I didn't do any running during that time, while I decided what to do with running and my life in 1957. But in my heart I knew I'd never give up running, and the continuous stream of notes I received from Jock buoyed me in that direction as well.

## Chapter Fourteen

"In 1957 I earned my dream to win Boston while standing behind the finish line holding a blanket for my boy."
–Jock Semple

YES, JOHNNY EXPERIENCED A big disappointment at Melbourne in the 1956 Olympics. As Jock put it, "After leading at the halfway point, he crapped out in the hundred-degree heat. I never say, 'the wall.' Nobody hits a wall; a man just gets pooped. After that Johnny wanted to give up running. But I hadn't trained him for ten years to have him quit. Johnny Kelley is the finest pure runner America has ever produced, and if his name hadn't been Johnny Kelley, if he'd had any other name in the phone book, his accomplishments would not have been confused with John the Elder's.

"Now, Young John would be given more credit for creating the line of college marathon runners in America that starts with himself and goes right up through Buddy Edelin in the early 1960s to Amby Burfoot, Kenny Moore, Frank Shorter, Bill Rodgers, Alberto Salazar, Craig Virgin and Greg Meyer in the late 1960s and into the 1970s and 1980s, and all the rest yet to come. Before Johnny, there was none of that. There were only us 'plodders,' as the papers referred to us."

Or, on days when newspapers were less generous, "Clowns in a parade."

In 1957 Johnny Kelley won the Boston Marathon, and Jock finally achieved his dream: to win Boston. He didn't win it as a runner, but he was a major player in Johnny's accomplishment.

By this time Jock had been in Boston a long time. Coffee cost nineteen cents a pound when he arrived in America in 1929. Milk cost ten cents, and Thom McAn sold shoes for four dollars. A new Packard automobile went for $2275 at Steven Fuller's on Commonwealth Avenue. Sears charged thirty dollars for a suit, and a cotton shirt went for $1.95. Those who were dapper, gents who walked up Beacon Street in top hats, put down thirteen cents for their Rockefeller cigars at smoke shops.

A year later, when Jock hitched from Philadelphia for his second Boston Marathon, he found that the prices of these items had, if anything, gone down. The Depression had hit, and everything deflated, especially people's hopes.

"Running helped me keep my spirits high," said Jock many years later. "I remember I wanted to win the 1934 Boston Marathon so badly. A rumor was circulating that the Finast Food Stores were hiring and I believed that winning at Boston would have given me stature enough to walk into the boss's office and propose to build him a championship running team. I was tired of working for eleven dollars a week. I was tired of sleeping on my brother's daybed. All people want their own lives, and I wanted mine."

It wasn't to be, but Jock pressed on. As the years passed Jock and Les Pawson spoke about the many changes they'd seen. Les had recently gone, in 1979, to New London to fire the starting gun at the John J. Kelley annual race that New London put on to honor Johnny each year.

"Since I have gained a measure of notoriety myself, they invited me and gave me a clean hotel room," said Jock.

Jock and Pawson laughed to think back over the days when motorists leaned out their cars and hollered, "Hey, you're gonna drop dead!"

"In those days, we went for weeks sometimes without seeing another runner. But it's changed, and I support expansion of the sport. Pawson agrees," said Jock. "It's so good to see people take an interest in remaining fit, and nothing works better for the waistline than sticking to a regular running schedule. Now, I'm not promoting another how-to lesson on the proper way to put one foot in front of the other. God knows there's enough of that advice on the shelves today, but I do believe that nearly all men and women can run. And, I believe guidance can be very helpful to those who wish to improve, and I think it's good for people who love our sport to know the history behind all the growth.

◆

Since Jock introduced qualifying times for the Boston Marathon (men must run below 2:50, women below 3:20, masters 3:10, and grand masters (over fifty) must run below 3:20) he felt it was only fair to offer hints on how to get the most out of the sport.

First, all runners should use their heads as well as their legs. If you're only 2:50 material, or 3:20, or four hours even, run at that speed and enjoy it. Leave the 2:09s to the 2:09 runners. Don't go busting up your family because you want to be Bill Rodgers. Do that and your wife will get frustrated with you after the beans have burned on the pot too many evenings. You'll be pushing your body through the wall, whatever new lingo they use, while the little lady's expected to have a PhD in carbohydrate loading.

"Look, I'm no model," Jock said, "but I do know what will get the wife's blood pressure up over two hundred. Run for the love of running, period. 'Amateur' comes from the Latin word *amator*, which means lover. Run because you love to run. There should be something left in the world where being in the race is prize enough in itself."

That brought Jock to his next point: amateur vs. professional running. "The money is pouring into this sport, and only a man with his face buried in his training flats can miss it. I sympathize with the runners," Jock said. "When you compare the salaries that athletes in other professional sports make in a year, it's a sin to think that a world-class runner would have to live on food stamps. But at the same time, I believe limits should be imposed, and I draw my line at Boston."

Jock never supported tinkering with the character of the Boston Marathon. During his time, organizers never had to pay a nickel to any one to get him or her to come to the race, yet runners still came. Something must pull them. Jock thought it was the tradition, the prestige that comes with competing in a race that has been run over the same course since 1897.

"With so many things changing today, I think the boys with their fat money pockets should invest in other races, if other race directors will have them, and leave bloody well enough alone at Boston," said Jock. "That's my stand, and if anybody disagrees, fine. But if you still think I might be a halfway nice man, you can come by my clinic for a rub. I charge ten dollars for the full treatment, that's massage, diathermy, hot box, whirlpool, shower, and that includes the towel. But if you can't afford it, then you pay me what you can spare. And if you're a runner, you might want to join the BAA, which I'm helping the younger fellas rebuild. That way you get the rubs for free.

"But even if you don't run, you might want to buy a t-shirt. I sell marathon t-shirts to fund the BAA. I promise they won't come up over your belly button after one washing."

One patient, the hot box guy, once mentioned an article in the paper, a story that said they were thinking of closing down the Garden. "Someday it may happen, Jock, the Bruins or Celtics might move to other quarters. You'd be out of a clinic," he said.

Jock remembered getting a strange card not long before. "A fella in New Hampshire sent a card to the BAA, to my 'successor,' the poor fool. The card read, I WAS SORRY TO HEAR THAT JOCK SEMPLE PASSED AWAY. HE DID A LOT TO KEEP THE BOSTON MARATHON A WORLD FAMOUS RACE AND NOT LET IT TURN INTO A CIRCUS. Now isn't that foolish? To send a card like that?"

"Why? To think that a man nearly eighty has succumbed, as we all must?" said the hot box guy.

"No, to think that the BAA could get someone to be my successor, to take this bloody phone. I never have claimed that I will go on forever. I'm not Tennyson's 'Brook' you know: 'Men may come and men may go, but I go on forever.' I don't believe they will ever close the Garden, but if I do get locked out, I'll take lessons and learn how to mope like an old man, which will come right after I wear a fur coat on the Fourth of July.

"So you're good with whatever happens, Jock?"

"I'm happy. I got my two dreams. I made the Olympics as a trainer for the US hockey team in 1948 and 1952, and now Kathrine Switzer tells me she is working to get me onto the 1984 team as a trainer for the women's marathon team. I've been behaving myself, angling for the job, maybe you have noticed how mellow I've become, but wouldn't that be a picture: the old fox smack in the coop with the chickens."

◆

Johnny Kelley never sought fame, which partially explains why the spotlight never caught him the way it has other running stars. Then again, the fifties were pre-boom days. Still, there was a time when Johnny received as many invitations to international races as Jock got phone calls. But he declined nearly every one. He might have used that exposure to build an international reputation for himself, but instead he stayed home for his family.

Johnny was always great with kids. For twenty-four years he taught high school, and they had to change his door hinges on his office constantly, since the kids wore them out. He lived in a Cape style house in Mystic with a garden in back, tall bushes out front (to obscure it from the bill collectors, he always said), and high school kids' jammed the driveway with their hot rods.

"Always the rebel, Johnny left teaching in 1980 because he was opposed to "the bureaucratic hassles," as Jock put it.

"Then he became a freelance writer," Jock said, "whatever the hell that means. But I have my suspicions that a locker room boy at the Y can show a fatter 1040 form at the end of the year. 'Sell your gold medals,' I told him. He doesn't display his medals and trophies. Not like me. He keeps them up in the attic in a box. 'Sell them,' I urged. He just laughed, then he biked off on a two-and-a-half-hour trip to some weekly newspaper office to deliver a poetry review that would earn him twenty-five dollars. By the time he got back, gold had risen to eight hundred dollars an ounce. Despite his not having one whit of business sense, the boy put America on the marathon map, though. That he did for sure!"

The forces that were to lead to the immense popularity running enjoys today were at work when Johnny ran 2:24 at the Rome Olympics in 1960, one minute slower than Emil Zatopek's

Olympic record set in 1952. But Rome belonged to an Ethiopian runner named Abebe Bilika who ran 2:15 barefoot over the Apian Way, and that evening the marathon became glamorous.

It would take Frank Shorter's winning the Olympic Marathon in 1972 before the glamour touched America, but nevertheless, change had been signaled. It was a long road from marathons in the 1930s to Shorter's win in 1972, but Johnny's 1957 Boston run was the pivotal event for the American marathon. That was the halfway point, it was as if Johnny took a stone and placed it down as the platform for Shorter and Rodgers to spring off of.

"And I was the happiest man alive to hold the blanket for him," said Jock.

◆

"The morning of April 20, 1957, Jock was more nervous than he ever had been in his life. For months he had been feeding news to the reporters in advance of that year's Boston Marathon.

"He's strong," Jock told the newspapermen.

He'd had to build up Johnny's confidence, the missing piece to the puzzle. Jock also had Johnny on the phone each night, as a way to shore him up. "Forget your hairbreadth loss to Viskari last year. You're the one," Jock told him. "Every foreign coach has asked me what you've been eating."

"They have?" Johnny exclaimed.

"They have," Jock said. Then he'd hang up, but Johnny, nervous as a cat on a griddle, would call back two minutes later for a clarification and a bit more reassurance.

"Don't worry," Jock told him night after night. "You're eating fine."

"But that morning I was so nervous my hands could barely

grip the wheel as I sat in my driveway in Lynn," said Jock. It was five-thirty A.M., and he was waiting for the car to warm up. "At the start in Hopkinton I bumped into Walter Brown, and he was worse. At about the twenty-one-mile mark, with Johnny leading, but pursued hotly by a host of foreigners, the press bus gave it gas and sped to the Lenox Hotel so we could have time to position ourselves at the finish line. I carried my wool army blanket and bounced on my toes at the line as Walter stood behind me."

"Think he can hold it?" Walter asked.

"Sure," Jock said, sweat pouring off his face. "He'll hold it!"

"You know, that's all I ever wanted," Walter said.

"I know," said Jock.

"It's all I have ever wanted, to see a BAA boy win the Boston Marathon."

"I know," Jock said, and Walter looked at him strangely.

"How do you know?"

"You told me that one day when you were lying on my rub-down table, Walter."

Walter smiled. "He had given me my clinic, and I had remembered. I could see that he was proud that I had remembered his secret wish in life," said Jock.

Suddenly there was a shout, then cheering, and Jock realized he had been turning his army blanket round and around like a corkscrew. Soon the whole corner of Commonwealth and Exeter exploded with applause, and Jock pushed off the shoulders of the fella in front of him to see over all the heads.

Applause rose now to the tops of the buildings and continued to build as thousands waited for a figure to appear, and in the midst of cheering that rolled over the crowd like a wave. Jock heard someone shout, "It's an American!" and he jumped up and down, then froze.

"Oh, my God!" Jock shouted. "Walter, he didn't eat a steak today, did he?"

◆

There is nothing like hearing about a Boston Marathon win directly from the runner himself, and Johnny's version is rich with detail.

Because Patriot's Day landed on Good Friday in 1957, the 61st Boston Athletic Association Marathon was bumped a day. Moving the celebration to Saturday probably didn't produce a ripple of emotion among the Commonwealth's two million citizens. But it did affect the 140 people who made up the field of the Marathon. Count me as one of them!

By two-twenty Saturday afternoon, I'd be thankful for the edge bumping the day to Saturday had given me. Yet, as the sun rose on April 20, I worried.Oh did I worry, that I had lost my edge. It was a strange worry born of a good night's sleep. Even a good sleep before the Boston could prove unnerving. My watch read four-forty-five. Outside, robins twittered. A warm spring day waited in the wings. Resting, I remembered Melbourne.

Melbourne, where I had led the Olympic Marathon for twelve miles in 85-degree heat before cramping up and walking. That twenty-first place had both pushed me to the brink of quitting running and challenged me to stay with it. Back home in Connecticut, I had brooded aloud. Maybe, just maybe, I'd have one more go at Boston, but I doubted if anybody thought I had a ghost of a chance."

"You'll do it. Just hang in. Melbourne was a fluke," my friend George Terry shored me up.

Most encouraging of my Boston friends was Jock. The fearsome Scot's vocabulary hid a dead spot, the spot where "quit" would be. "Oh Johnny, fer cripes sakes, yer gain' t'win at Boston in a great foreign field."

That confidence fired me up in 1957's opening months of cold and slush.

So the night before the race I lay and reflected in Laura Harlow's guest bed in Arlington, just north of Boston, in the house where John Kelly the Elder and Laura, his fiancé, had invited Jessie and me to stay the night before the big race. Beside me, Jessie slept undisturbed. A marathoner's wife has to be immune to insomnia. How many other young fellows thereabouts had popped wide awake at four-forty-five, worrying about the possibility of having slept off their edge?

"All 140," my wife could have told you.

Soon I heard a discreet tapping at my door. Then a voice. "Hey kid." Old Kel was up at the crack of dawn. "Sleep okay?"

"Sure, John, slept fine. Sorta."

"Want to sneak out for a little stretch on the grass?"

"Be right with you," I said.

At age forty-nine, John A. Kelley was Boston's King of the Road. The wiry Edison Company employee had won the BAA race twice, in 1935 and 45, and placed second seven times. On Belmont Golf Course's sunny slopes, early bird golfers saluted him as the legend he was.

"Go get 'em today, Kel!" they shouted.

"Thanks, pal," he answered them, teasing, "Don't forget my son here," he teased. Who'd have believed the two Johnny Kelleys of the Boston Marathon were unrelated?

Back in the house, the women had prepared a breakfast of grapefruit, scrambled eggs, toast a plenty, and honey coffee. At nine o'clock, dishes done, we two Johnny's double-checked our gear and piled into the car for the twenty-mile drive to Hopkinton.

The Revolutionary War-redolent suburb typically welcomed the marathon invasion with a kind of subdued colonial revelry. Militiamen and dames mingled with motley marathoners, and a freshening west wind carried scents of musket powder and rubbing lotion.

In 1957, nobody could have foreseen a day when Hopkinton would be closed to the public at nine A.M. on Patriot's Day. In 1957, only the runners themselves were to be corralled. At eleven-thirty, the entire field was herded into a snow fence enclosure on the green.

Inside, officials commenced calling out and checking off names and numbers, and I finally caught my first look at the formidable foreigners. I saw Finns Veikko Karvonena and Olavi Manninen. (Karvonen had won in 1954 and was favored by most today.) I saw Koreans Soong Chil Han and Ching Woo Lim. (Koreans had won both of the races they had entered since 1947.) I saw Japanese Keizo Yamada and Nobuyoshi Sadanga. (Yamada had won in 1953.) I also saw Pedro Peralta of Mexico, and my friend and fellow Olympian, Gordon Dickson of Canada. As I surveyed my competition, I wondered who was the foreigner, me or they!"

Looking to chat away the endless minutes before the start, I found my good friends George Terry an Rudolpho Mendez. Together, we made an American team as strong as any of the foreigners. One of us might even win it today. We all knew that, but it would have been unconscionable to speak it. After all, no American had won at Boston since John A. Kelley had prevailed in 1945, twelve lean years earlier.

George came up on it. "Lads," he began, "I think one of us will take it."

Rudolpho and I listened like fidgety school kids.

"Thing is, we have to decide who has the best chance. Then two of us are going to have to set it up for him."

George was proposing that Americans run like Finns, Koreans, and Japanese. In truth, I was too nervous to pay close attention to George's proposal. I did favor it on the principle of giving back some of what had been heaped on all of us over the years. Today our foreign friends would have three Americans to watch out for instead of the usual one.

At eleven-fifty the corral gate was breached. The herd moved out, kicking and bellowing. At high noon BAA President Walter Brown fired a sawed-off shotgun heavenward, and the 1957 stampede was on.

Easter Saturday, 1957, did everything right. Puff-ball cumulus clouds decorated the blue sky, and the temperature reached the upper sixties. Afterward, Yamada would blame the "hot, hot weather" for his sixth place finish. Right off the mark, I knew the weather was just right for me!

The field quickly shook down. By Ashland, two miles, those who would make the top ten ran easily in a leading pack. Eyes moved warily. Nobody wanted to ask outright, "How's the pace, friends?" Framingham, six-and-a-half miles. The order held. George, Rudy, and I ran bunched within the larger group.

A huge Rising Sun flag greeted the runners near the checkpoint. Exhortations in Finnish boomed from the van that attended Karvonen and Manninen. Tiny American flags bobbed everywhere: GO, AMERICANS!

We met more of the same at the Natick ten-mile checkpoint, and the crowds swelled with each suburban milestone.

A year ago, George Terry had set records at the Framingham and Natick checkpoints, only to drop out. Today he ran coolly in the lead pack, and I could see his presence troubling the taciturn Finns. They traded glances repeatedly, catching the American trio in-between.

Again, however, George was forced to read the handwriting on the road. Leaving Natick, he admitted to painful blisters. "In a mile or so, guys, I'm gonna fall back a bit. Keep teaming them, and, near Wellesley decide who's able to go for it."

"I can win today!" I wanted to burst out. But it was too early to chance that utterance. What a pick me up those Wellesley College coeds gave us. What a lovely halfway marker. I was still running effortlessly as the coeds cheered us. Rudolpho sensed how strong I felt.

"Hey Johnny, how long can you hold this pace?"

"Another fifteen miles if I have to," I told him truthfully. "How about you?"

"I don't know. I'm going to have to slow down a little, I think. We're on a 2:20 pace. Too fast for me."

Fourteen miles. I was the last little Indian. Only Finns and Koreans remained of the foreign contingent in the lead pack, and spectators kept us informed: "No Japanese in sight!" the crowd shouted.

For the past several checkpoints, the accompanying press bus had been unable to disgorge its passengers before the leaders ran through. Jock occupied a right rear seat on that bus, unable to get me the sponges and oranges he had filled his pockets with. At Newton Lower Falls, sixteen miles, he leapt from the still-moving vehicle.

"Johnny! How are you feelin'?"

"Terrific, Jock! I can't believe it!"

"Here, mop yer brow," he said.

I caught the water-soaked sponge. Jock paced me while I traded the sponge for an orange slice. Then up came the first of the Newton Hills, and Karvonen forced the pace. He didn't look comfortable though. I followed, but the tactic shook Manninen, Lim, and Han, and we never saw them after that.

On these hills three years earlier, Karvonen had run Jim Peters rubber-legged. Making the same move on me today, he looked a trifle rubbery himself. In every struggle there comes a turning point.

For me, in the 1957 Boston Marathon, the turning point came as Karvonen and I raced along Commonwealth Avenue in Newton and thousands cheered in sunshine for an American winner. I was now alone in the race with the Finnish champion, the two of us running stride for stride. Either I made a decisive break here and ran a nine-mile gamble to the finish, or I waited for him to crack somewhere down the line.

I decided to gamble. Up the second Newton Hill, I quickened my pace about ten seconds per mile. Karvonen's footfalls fell away and I could hear his labored breathing after his steps were no longer audible. I topped infamous Heartbreak Hill full of running! Boston College. Five downhill miles to the Exeter Street finish. It was all roses. The great crowd dinned out all other sounds."

Jock bruised his right hand pounding on the press bus outside wall. "There's nobody in sight!" he yelled as the bus made its last zig-zag around me on Beacon Street, Brookline.

At Kenmore Square, I finally believed the dream. I was about to win Boston, yes, I was about to win Boston!

I eased enough to savor the last mile home.

I remember catching a glimpse of Jock as I pummeled down Exeter Street over those last delicious yards toward the finish. He was opening and closing his arms with the blanket. Behind him I saw Walter Brown, beaming also and I was happy for both of them. As I crossed the line, our eyes met and we were all smiling. Years later, so many Bostons between then and now, I realized we made a triangle.

After the race, Mayor Hynes crowned me with the laurel wreath. Jock swaddled me in his army blanket. My wife kissed me. Reporters, who for once could ask their questions without need for an interpreter, cheered.

A flood of feet have washed down the pike since Easter Saturday, 1957 and the Boston Marathon has grown to a reality beyond Jock's wildest dreams.

I don't regret having passed down the road too soon. It was enough to know that I was part of something special, a contributor along the long line; for, as Ernest Hemingway wrote, "Nothing is ever really finished. Nothing really ends."

## One More Jock Story

"I love Jock like a grandfather. I've learned how to get
his dander up. I have a proven method: I disagree
with him. It works every time."
–Patti Catalano

WHEN PATTI RETURNED TO Jock's clinic following her run with her
husband Joe, she hardly said boo. That was completely out of character. Usually Patti was quite animated, but now she avoided Jock's
eyes —and he knew why.

"You think I'm going to scold you, don't you?" he asked.

"I just went a little extra, Jock, a few extra miles," she said.

"About fifty miles extra. Tell me, what's Providence like? Do
they still have the big white capitol building in the middle of town?"

"Jock, I'm sorry if I kept you waiting."

"It's not me, Patti. It's my men. I put four of them back out
onto the street about ten o'clock with their hair wet and shirt tails
out. I sent them to the hamburger joint, but one fella came back
about five minutes ago, and I told him to go eat another chili dog.
Poor Mickey. How many chili dogs can a man eat?"

"I'm sorry, Jock. I try."

"Give you an inch, and you take the extra miles."

Patti laughed. For once she didn't get into a good-natured tangle with Jock, a conflict of their strong personalities. Patti removed her sweat suit and climbed up onto Jock's rubdown table in her running outfit. Jock had sent all his male patients away for an hour in anticipation of her return. They had been "banished." That was the rule. Jock's "cash customers," as he called his male clientele, understood that on Tuesdays Jock did not take patients between eleven o'clock and noon. He reserved that time for Patti.

Jock and Patti had been friends for years, ever since she had joined his BAA. Given the circumstances of their first meeting, however, one might have suspected the opposite.

Their first meeting was not auspicious, reflective of their strong personalities colliding. "I rode in Jock's car during a race so I could watch Joe run. Joe said it would be okay to be in the car with Jock," said Patti. "Still, I thought to myself, *Oh, Geez!* I knew Jock's reputation in advance. I knew he had chased Kathrine Switzer in 1967. Anyway, Joe said it would be all right. Then at one point in the race Jock stopped his car to give water to his BAA runners, and I got out behind him. As he gave water to Joe, I snapped Joe's picture, and Jock turned on me. 'Don't bother the runners!' he shouted, and I thought, *Oh, Geez! Here I am getting into a fight with this guy*, but I didn't say anything. Then we stopped again, and I got out to take another picture. 'Don't bother the runners, let them concentrate,' Jock barked again, and this time I barked back. 'I'll do what I damn well please!' I couldn't believe it, that I had talked back to him, but I didn't like anyone yelling at me."

Jock just stood, staring at me, as if he'd been kissed between the eyes with a two-by-four. "Needless to say," Patti said, "we didn't talk in the car after that." A month later they met again when Jock asked Joe to bring "the girl who's been running so well," up to the clinic. He wanted to get her to join the BAA.

Jock did not know he had asked to meet the young woman he had chauffeured in the car that day. He didn't know who he was asking to see. He knew only the rumors. Stories had begun circulating around New England that a young woman from Quincy had run 2:53 in her first marathon attempt. In addition, she had been running only five and a half months and had just quit smoking, yet still managed to run sub-three hours in her first race.

"She's injured," Joe said, seeking to prevent a confrontation.

"All the better," Jock said. "What's her problem?"

"She's got a sore hip."

"Bring her by, I'll fix her up," Jock said, in the famous Jock fashion that left no room for debate.

"I was terrified," Patti said. "I'd never had a rubdown before. Plus, I had fought with the guy. Anyway I walked in, about two steps behind Joe, and didn't say a word."

The instant Jock saw me, he recognized me. But he didn't say a word.

"I walked over and climbed up on his table," Patti said. "Then he started probing my calf with his fingers. That's the remarkable thing about Jock. When it hurt someplace, he went someplace else and dug in with his fingers. I said, "Yeeeeow!""

That broke the ice. "Jock started talking a blue streak, and so did I," Patti said. "He told me he had nothing against women runners, only those who break the rules, who 'b-o-t-h-e-r' the runners during a race."

"Look," I said, "I don't want to be a welder, or a construction worker. I don't want to be like men, I just want to run." He found another sore spot and I went, "Yow!"

But when Patti got up off that table, she could walk again.

The friendship grew. While wearing the BAA colors Patti became the top American female marathon runner. In 1980, at the

New York Marathon, she became the first American woman to break 2:30. NBC News did a spot on her that night, and as she beamed into the camera, Patti said to millions, as if looking into Jock's eyes: "I did this for Jock. For his birthday present."

Jock was watching TV that night. He never admitted it around the clinic, but a tear rolled down his cheek.

Patti Catalano, one in a long line of BAA stars (following in the tradition of John J. Kelley and Bill Rodgers), explained her relationship with Jock very succinctly.

"We didn't talk about how much we cared about each other," she said. "But we felt it."

## Epilogue

Yes, Jock Semple scared the livin' bejesus out of Kathrine Switzer in the 1967 Boston Marathon. Yes, the horrific photo was emblazoned across the front pages and sports pages of countless newspapers around the globe. Yes, readers everywhere reacted with appropriate shock and outrage.

Now, let's add a few more points. Yes, the photo became a clarion call for the advancement of women's running. Yes, Kathrine Switzer used Jock himself and that 1967 photo of her to promote the women's marathon as an important new event in the Olympic Games.

You see where this is going? No Jock, and maybe no women's Olympic Marathon. At least not for many years beyond 1984.

More important, few today understand the history, context, and intent of Semple's furious charge after Switzer. He wasn't trying to harm her. He had no outsized gripe against women running the Boston Marathon. He hadn't chased down Bobbi Gibb the previous year, and wouldn't fly after the handfuls of women who ran Boston in subsequent years (before women were allowed to enter officially for the first time in 1972).

Semple was solely focused on the now famous number, 261, that Switzer wore on her sweatshirt. In 1967, Amateur Athletic Union rules prohibited women from running any officially sanctioned long-distance races, such as the Boston Marathon. While Semple held no exalted title with the Boston Marathon—he wasn't president or chief executive or even race director—he was something more important: the guy who cared more than anyone else, and did all the work. Without him, it was impossible to imagine a smooth-running Boston Marathon.

As the registration, course management, and results guy, Semple felt it his duty to uphold what he called, in a Scottish burr that no written words can capture, "the r-r-rules and r-r-regulations." The AAU ruled with monolithic power, and sat at the right hand of the International Olympic Committee. If the AAU decreed that women could not register for a long-distance race and compete with an official race number, well, then it was Semple's job to administer and police this directive.

Several miles into the 1967 Marathon, Semple heard from photographers on the press vehicle that they had spotted a woman running the course, as the book you've just read tells so explicitly. She was behind Gibb, running in her second straight Boston, and would have mattered little except for one minor detail: She was wearing an official race number, just like the one Semple had passed out to about seven hundred male runners that morning.

Not that it was a fancy number, or covered by corporate logos as today's numbers are. No, it was a nothing number. It had nothing on it save black ink over a white background. But as far as Semple was concerned, it was practically a holy relic, because it was a Boston Marathon number.

And you bet your life, he meant to maintain its sanctity. That's why he jumped off the press bus and tore down the road—as you read—face contorted in a vicious snarl, in an attempt to reach Switzer and rip off her number. If he had succeeded, he would have stopped and walked slowly back to the press bus, fully satisfied. He would have left Switzer alone. So long as he had the number, and she didn't.

It all started with Jock Semple. Photo by David Keith for *Runner's World*, and initially published in their April 1987 issue.

Jock (left) and Will Cloney, Boston Marathon director, are widely credited with keeping the Boston Marathon "alive" through the 1950s and into the 1980s. Image courtesy of the estate of Jock Semple.

Jock (right) reconnects with life-long friend and mentor "Bricklayer" Bill Kennedy, winner of the 1917 Boston Marathon. Image courtesy of the estate of Jock Semple.

John J. Kelley (the Younger) was "America's only hope" at the
Boston Marathon each year in the 1950s. Image courtesy of the
estate of John J. Kelley.

Emil Zatopek (left) and John J. Kelley on a practice track at the Melbourne, Australia Olympic Games in 1956. Image by Global Olympic Picture Association, and courtesy of the estate of John J. Kelley.

Right: John J. Kelley (the Younger) during the "glory days" of Jock's BAA marathon team. Image courtesy of the estate of John J. Kelley.

Jock (left), with John J. Kelley (the Younger) on the Yonkers finish line after winning the National Marathon title. Image courtesy of the estate of John J. Kelley.

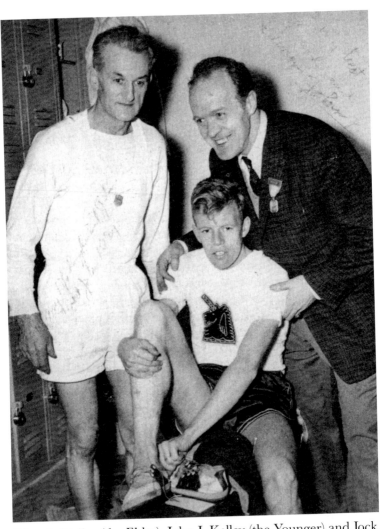

John A. Kelley (the Elder), John J. Kelley (the Younger) and Jock. Image courtesy of the estate of John J. Kelley.

Jock (left) helps John J. Kelley (the Younger) after he won the Boston Marathon in 1957. Image courtesy of the estate of John J. Kelley.

"Now look at this: Does it look like I'm saying 'Get the hell on the bus?' *I'm always civil!*" Image courtesy of the estate of Jock Semple.

Rodney K. McNichol's cartoon in the *Boston Globe* paints a different picture! Image from the collection of Rodney K. McNichol.

It's been called "The Great Shove!" Jock (right) chases "K.V. Switzer" down the road in the 1967 Boston Marathon to get "his" number back. The event effectively helped usher in women's running in America when the photo landed on front pages around the world. Image by Don Robinson, and courtesy of United Press International.

Above: Despite a rocky start, Jock (right) and Kathrine Switzer eventually became friends. "Come on, Lassie," he said at the start of the 1973 Boston Marathon—after the rules had been changed to permit women to compete. "Let's get ourselves a wee bit of notoriety!" he added. Then he gave her a hug and the crowd cheered! Photo courtesy of *Runners World*.

Left: Today Kathrine is a global advocate for women's running, and founder of "261 Fearless," an empowerment nonprofit.

"Pour it on, lad. They couldn't catch you if they had" roller skates!" Jock called to Bill Rodgers in 1975 as Bill streaked to his first Boston Marathon victory. Photo from the *Boston Globe*.

Above: Bill Rodgers (who is wearing number 1) competes in one of his four victorious Boston Marathons during his reign as "King of the Roads." Image courtesy of the Bill Rodgers collection.

Right: Amby Burfoot, 1968 Boston Marathon winner and nationally renowned writer, was introduced to running by John J. Kelley, his high school teacher. Amby also roomed with Bill Rodgers when they were in college. Photo credit: Nancy Nessiff.

Artwork by Phil Bissell, *Boston Globe*.

Jock's BAA team, led by John J. Kelley (the Younger,) took first, second and fourth in the Pan American Games in 1959. Above: Jim Roy, founder of the John J. Kelley Memorial Fund, at the unveiling of the "Kelley Statue" in Mystic, CT, Kelley's hometown, in 2014.

Former Boston Marathon winners at the unveiling, left to right: Geoff Smith, Amby Burfoot, Sara Mae Berman, Bill Rodgers, Nina Kuscsik and Jack Fultz.

**Every sip** takes us a step
closer to **curing lung cancer!**

This edition of *Just Call Me Jock* is published by the Barb's Beer Foundation, producer of Barb's Beer. The foundation raises funds to cure non-smoker's lung cancer in the name of Barb Murphy, wife of Jock's biographer, Tom Murphy. Barb passed away from lung cancer in 2013. Tom's proceeds from this edition go to the Barb's Beer Foundation to bring Barb's Beer to Boston following success of a similar campaign in Seattle.

Above left: Barb crosses the finish line in the 2000 Boston Marathon. Her silhouette from the race that day serves as the logo for Barb's Beer. Learn more about Barb's Beer and the Racing to the Cure campaign to cure lung cancer, which increasingly afflicts women, at BarbsBeer.org.

Semple believed in upholding the AAU's dominion, but even more so in maintaining the status of the Boston Marathon as a serious, world-class competition. That Boston might have been considered anything else is hard to imagine today. However, runners and marathoners were far from esteemed citizens in the mid-1960s.

Believe me, I was there, and I vividly remember. I suffered the same onslaughts as anyone else. You didn't have to be a woman runner to feel caught in the cross-hairs. While I was training in my hometown in the 1960s, cars would slow down alongside me for precisely three reasons: 1) to ask directions; 2) to hurl a beer can in my direction; or 3) to utter a stupid epithet, ranging from the obscene, to "what are you doing running around town in your underwear?" (I'm not counting the time a local politician pulled up next to me, shoved a thick sheath of propaganda flyers my way, and asked me to distribute them at the front door of every house I ran past.)

It was no different in Boston itself. There, every April, the sports writers enjoyed typing their little pun: "It must be spring, the saps are running again." You heard it from Jock in his "boooook," as he called it, marathoners were not heroes to ourselves or anyone else. Too small, too skinny, too timid, not skilled at football, basketball, hockey or baseball, we felt like outcasts.

We had just the Boston Marathon; it was our Super Bowl. And Jock Semple was the promoter and referee in-chief—the only person determined to preserve and enhance its heritage.

When Gibb, Switzer, and other women began running Boston, sure, Semple regarded them with some skepticism. He worried that they might be "clowns or publicity seekers," the worst words he could apply to anyone wishing to run Boston. He soon changed his tune; he saw up close that the pioneer women runners had trained hard and were serious about the marathon challenge.

When the AAU declared that women could run Boston offi-cially in 1972, Semple was all in. He realized that well-trained women runners could only add to the status and fame of his cher-ished event.

Best of all, Semple's efforts maintained the class and integrity of the Boston Marathon. When it was time for women to be re-ceived more fully, Boston was waiting for them, and they could count on running a world-class event.

They could also count on Semple's support. When Switzer improved to a 2:51 in 1975, he was there cheering for her. When Joan Benoit won in 1979 and 1983, Semple nodded his approval. She was, after all, a New England road runner—his favorite species.

If Semple were alive today to watch the twelve thousand plus women finishers at the Boston Marathon, he would certainly shake his head in disbelief at what he, Kathrine Switzer, and many others have wrought.

And then he would summon up that Scottish burr to say, "Those gals can r-r-really r-r-run."

—Amby Burfoot, editor at large, *Runner's World*, and 1968 Boston Marathon winner

## The Barb's Beer Foundation

This has been a story about Jock and his impact on the course of women's running, unwitting certainly, but real. On its own merits Jock's story (and his wonderful father/son relationship with Johnny Kelley) deserves to be made available to a new generation of runners, especially women runners.

But, retelling this story also offers an opportunity to highlight the special passion of a particular woman runner, Barbara Murphy. Barb never challenged for a place among the top finishers at Boston, but she did reflect the spirit of "grit" exemplified by Jock throughout his tale. She also reflected the grit of all of the women runners who have joined this sport since Kathrine Switzer made her oh-so-memorable debut. Barbara was part of that long, long parade of women runners, having run the Boston Marathon in 2000 as a fiftieth birthday present to herself.

But this book has a higher purpose. As noted in the Introduction, we (Barb's friends and family) created Barb's Beer and the Racing to the Cure campaign to continue Barb's "run" toward the goal she set for herself after she developed non smoker's lung cancer in 2007. Her goal was, and ours is, to help find a cure for lung cancer. Barb fought the disease valiantly before she passed away in 2013. Her passion to call attention to this disease and find a cure so no one else gets it consumed the latter portion of her life.

Lung cancer is the single greatest killer of women, so we have seized upon one of Jock's mantras: "Seize opportunity." We are seizing this opportunity to bring *Just Call Me Jock* out as a tie-in to our efforts to expand Barb's Beer to Boston. We are so proud that it has already established a successful base in Seattle, and throughout much of the Pacific Northwest.

The Barb's Beer Foundation, which produces Barb's Beer, is a 501c3 charity that was created in 2014. The foundation is also the publisher of this new edition of *Just Call Me Jock*. The author share of profits from the book will go toward efforts to bring Barb's Beer and the Racing to the Cure campaign to Boston, and ultimately to Massachusetts, as a prelude to national expansion. All publisher profits will also go toward the cause.

Barb would like that, I'm certain, since the more successful Barb's Beer becomes, the more funds we will be able to generate to support GRACE (cancerGRACE.org), the charity created by Dr. Howard West, Barb's oncologist and one of our country's leading experts on lung cancer. He is working very hard to find a cure.

Beer is a fitting vehicle for this cause, since Barb was a beer lover, as was my co-author, Johnny Kelley, who often said to me whenever he wanted to catch up. "Call me when you get to town, Tom, we'll grab some 'Gansetts," meaning Narragansett Beer. Not only did Johnny know Barb, but he loved her, as she did him. Johnny, ever the fluid editor, would be happy to change his tune from 'Gansetts" to "Call me when you get to town and we'll get some Barbs!" Of that, I'm sure! Jock did not drink beer, but he would have approved of our campaign too, I have no doubt, as he also knew Barb.

The logo for Barb's Beer is a silhouette of Barb crossing the finish line at the 2000 Boston Marathon, and the tag line below the logo is: Every sip takes us a step closer to curing lung cancer." Curing lung cancer is a marathon, and we plan to make Barb's Beer a strong runner in that race.

Thank you for your support of this book and thank you in advance for your support for Barb's Beer and our Racing to the Cure campaign. Look for the beer, a great tasting American Pale Ale, at a tavern near you. If you know someone who owns a tavern and may want to put Barb's on tap, let us know through our website at barbsbeer.org. You can also make a donation in support of the cause at barbsbeer.org/donate.

Onward and upward, as we race to the cure!

—Tom Murphy

## Acknowledgements

Yes, it takes a village, but one of the things that distinguished Jock during his tenure as co-director of the Boston Marathon from the late 1940s into the 1980s was how much of the work he did himself. He was tireless, and this book is a tribute to Jock for his devotion to the race he loved so much.

On the other hand, an author's work depends on others, and though Jock Semple and Johnny Kelley, my co-authors, are no longer with us—Jock having passed from cancer in 1988 and Johnny from lung cancer in 2011—I know they would wants me to acknowledge the many wonderful people who made it possible for us to re-publish *Just Call Me Jock*, which first appeared in 1982.

First, I want to thank Gloria Ratti, vice president of the Boston Athletic Association, who offered immediate support when I told her of my idea to bring this book back out for another generation. I first met Gloria in 1973 when I ran neighborhood road races in Boston, and she was the lady who held the stop watch and gave us our times. She knew Barb, and when I told her I wanted to bring the Jock book back to raise funds to bring our Racing to the Cure campaign to Boston to help cure lung cancer, she was all in.

I also want to thank Amby Burfoot, who is a giant in the running community, and a giant in terms of his giving spirit. Amby offers the Introduction from the original book, as well as an Epilogue in this edition. I want to thank Jim Roy, head of the John Kelley Memorial Fund, who led the campaign to create a statue for Johnny in Mystic, Massachussetts. Jim runs stride for stride with Amby in terms of generosity.

As for the runners who supported our effort, both the original book and this edition, Billy Rodgers heads the pack, as he did so often in races. Also I want to thank Kathrine Switzer, who is a seminal character in Jock's life, as he is in hers. Kathrine's tireless devotion to the cause of women's running has always impressed me immensely. Thank you also to Guy Morse, former Boston Marathon race director, for his twenty-eight years service to the race.

Thank you also to Johnny's daughters, Julia, Kathleen and Eileen, who were young women when Johnny and I first embarked upon our task to bring Jock's story to life in the 1980s. Now all have all grown into impressive ladies.

On the writerly side, there is no greater editor than Lisa Wysocky, who along with my agent, Sharlene Martin, have always been front and center with support.

I also want to thank Ryan Goelzenleuchter for his efforts with graphic design. Thank you also to Tom Morante and his colleagues at Holland and Knight, Michael Newman, Howard Wayne, and Ruthe Canter. They played a pivotal role on the legal end (pro bono) along with John O'Connor and Joe Crowley in helping us bring Barb's Beer to Massachusetts. And on that note, kudos also to Fr. Isaac and Ron Carlson of Spencer Brewery, and the Trappist Monks for being our partner in that effort.

Thank you must also go to the "team" from Don Bosco and the "team" from Regis College, Barb's alma mater, for their support for Racing to the Cure, and to Chuck Hohing for creating the recipe for Barb's Beer. Thanks also to Pat Robertson and Trish Manley for their support.

Johanne Connors, Barb's sister, and her husband, Terry, have been tireless in their work to build a network of restaurant partners, a cornerstone for success. I thank them along with Andy and Jane Murphy, owners of the Lost Dog Pub, Peggy Murphy, Jan Clark, Mike Dunford, Mike Barretti, and Janine Wert.

My love has no bounds for our daughter, Caitlin, and her husband, Justin, for their leadership with this project and our foundation. Special thanks to Dr. Howard West for all he gave Barb, and to his colleagues at GRACE (cancerGRACE.org). Thank you to Denise Brock and Carlea Bauman for their support, and to other project leaders including in the northwest, including John Blethen, Maura Ball, Dan Bothman, Suz Gavin, Mike Mackley, Hayley Black, Joe Fugere, Amy French, Pete Lachapelle, Kurt Ahrens, Janet Lightner, Ed Bennet, Bryan Bendix and Bryan Krueger.

I must also send a thank you to members of the Bogmen, PJ O'Connor and Brendan and Billy Ryan, for producing our Barb's Beer song, "Racing to the Cure," and to Hector and Cathy Murphy, Mark Longo, Bob Hamecs, and Sander Flaum for fundraising support, as well as to Paul and Anthony Ramirez, Mary Liz Murphy and my Murphy siblings.

Thank you to Peggy Peters Fox whom I peppered with ideas, and who never flagged, to Barrie Brett and Doug McCormick for always being there, and to Pamela Steenland for her texted "pings" of support.

Finally, I want to thank Joan Kenney. When I ran the Boston Marathon in 2016 to call attention to this project, she kept my sweats and when I made her wait oh-so-long to give them back, she never complained.

Thank you all.

# The Last 385 Yards

Through the years Jock developed a special relationship with many of America's top athletes. Thousands of men and women passed through Boston Garden each year, and many took special care to pass through Jock's clinic. The following stories represent the recollections of a small sampling of the people who were served by Jock.

Some are athletes, others are life-long friends. In a large way their favorite memories of the man add to Jock's portrait, and testify to the mark he left on their lives and on sport in Boston.

**Kathrine Switzer**
**Director of Avon Sports Programs Worldwide**
Do I remember the moment I made up with Jock (after he tried to pull me out of the Boston Marathon)? The instant we became good friends? Sure, I remember. He kissed me.

Two steps led up to that happy incident. Of course I didn't talk to Jock in 1968 or 1969, as I was terrified to come back to Boston. Two words described Jock in 1967: instant mad. But I did run [illegally] again in 1970. I didn't see Jock, though. The press bus passed us and I knew he was in there, but I didn't see him. I didn't dare look up as the bus passed.

Then in 1972, the first year women were permitted to run in the Boston Marathon, Jock and I came face to face. He had made the announcement about our eligibility that spring in very polite but cold terms. "The women are permitted to run," he said. "And I wish them good luck."

Just like that. Like ice.

I placed third in the women's division in 1972, and in the Prudential afterward, I went to get my trophy. Jock made the presentation, and reporters and photographers crammed into a pack in front. Silence fell on the room as I walked to the platform and Jock waited with my award—only it was broken. The figurine at the top had broken off and Jock was very sweet as he told me I should send it back to him, that he would see I got a new one. I said thank you, but as I went to take the trophy and step off the platform, Jock said loudly, in that rapid-fire way he talked, "I've been mad at you for five years and I'm still mad and you *deserve* a broken trophy!"

Everybody cracked up, and that was the first sign of a thaw.

The next year we made up completely. I wrote a letter to him after Boston in 1972 telling him how much I appreciated the hard work he and Will Cloney put in each year, and how much I appreciated the chance to run and how happy I was to get a trophy. But I didn't get a response from him. I didn't know if he was still on the warpath or what.

He was still mad at Arnie Briggs, I knew that. Arnie had been a running buddy of Jock's in the old days. That is, before Arnie trained me for my Boston race in 1967. I had met Arnie at Syracuse. He was a mailman, and he instructed me when I was brand new to marathon running. Jock called him a "co conspirator" but I swear to this day, I did not intentionally set out to break the rules. I put K. V. Switzer on my application because that's how I wrote my name. That's how I signed all documents, even my checks.

Jock never believed that. To him I was a cheat. "The girl didn't run the race," he said in 1967. "She only ran the same course as the men."

When I didn't hear from him after I wrote my long letter in 1972, I assumed he was still mad. Then I saw him.

You know how Jock was at the starting line of the Boston Marathon? He literally picked people up if they were out of place and hurled them into the air. Boston 1973 was no different. I was standing at the front of the starting line, where they placed all the women, and I could hear Jock looking for people with high numbers. I could hear him coming. "AAAAggghh!" I could hear him saying, and I put my head down. I heard him come closer and then I heard footsteps right behind me. "AAAAggghh!" he said as he came up behind my shoulder, and I turned. I was scared to death, but he was smiling. He put his face right up beside mine, cheek to cheek, and he said, loudly enough for everyone to hear,

"Come on, lass. Let's get ourselves a wee bit of no-tor-EYE-eteeeee!" and he kissed me. Fat on the cheek.

The cameras clicked like mad, and Jock and I have been best friends ever since.

### Bud Collins
### Sports Columnist and Television Commentator

One day during the National Doubles Tennis Championships at Longwood Cricket Club in 1967, Jock saved John Newcombe's life (according to Newcombe). Not his biological life, just his life in the National Doubles Championship, which shouldn't be belittled.

Here's how it happened. Newcombe woke up the morning of August 29 and could not walk. With his and Tony Roche's big match set to be played against Owen Davidson and Bill Bowery in a few hours, Newcombe was in a state. Quickly, he called Jock.

Something was pressing on Newcombe's sciatic nerve, Jock said, and he went to work as Newcombe lay stretched out on the master's portable table at courtside. "Jock gave me heat treatments and a heavy massage," Newcombe said. "When I stood up again I could walk."

Newcombe and Roche's 6-8, 9-7, 6-3, 6-3 decision over David-son and Bowery assured the young Australians of a fourth jewel in a crown worn only by three teams before them.

### Terry O'Reilly
### Veteran Boston Bruins Winger

I didn't know what to expect when the Bruins' trainer sent me to "The Boston Garden Laboratory," as he called it, to be repaired after I sprained my ankle very badly in a game. The team trainer had exhausted all his remedies and, having failed to produce a cure, shuffled me down the hall behind the Celtics' offices to Jock.

Quickly, Jock fixed me up, and saved the trainer the embarrassment of the coach getting on his back, but even more than the therapy, I enjoyed Jock's stories that day. Even ten or more years later I prided myself that I could get Jock started on a cantankerous riff. All I needed to do was mention the Boston Marathon, and he launched into a history of the event. Or, he descried "the blasted phone," or the "cheats," or "Rosie Ruiz," who jumped into the race and into the lead in 1980. The results of my random tests confirmed a close link between Jock's best stories and his worst massages.

As long as I can remember, Jock traveled with our Bruins team in the playoffs. On one such trip, the night before a big game, I couldn't sleep. I had playoff jitters and called Jock. I woke him up and told him how bad off I was. He told me he'd be right down, and he rushed over immediately with his portable table to give me a massage. The next morning, he asked how I felt.

"'Great!' I said, and I told him I was ready for the hat trick.

"'Fantastic," he said. "Now that justifies my existence."

Score one for Jock.

### John Kelley (the Elder)
### Fifty-Year BAA Marathon Veteran

One night in the 1930s Jock and I nearly got in a row with a bunch of sailors in New London, Connecticut. I guess they had a few cold ones in them and they couldn't sleep, or pass out, or whatever. They thought we were making too much racket. I guess we were. Jock and I were kids in the thirties and we used to cut up a lot.

The incident occurred in New London on Thanksgiving morning. Jock and I had gone down to Connecticut for a fifteen-mile race. We stayed at the YMCA, in a dollar-a-night room, which was our custom. At night we were making noise, as kids do, and the sailors got the idea that we skinny fellas were not behaving properly. In walked a couple of brawny sailors. One word from them and we piped right down. Wouldn't you?

Jock has always given freely of himself. Sure, he can get obstreperous. I once saw him go to a group of bagpipe players at a race and tell them to be quiet. "I don't care if you're Scottish," he told them. "I love all the Scottish, and I love your music, but you're making a racket and screwing things up so I can't get race results."

Jock would do anybody a favor in a minute. Even if he was obstreperous. But they'd better not be musicians and make too much racket. Maybe Jock learned too well from the sailors. If I hadn't known him so well, I'd say the sailors changed his life.

## Bob Cousy
### NBA Hall of Famer, Boston Celtic Great

For years Jock did his magic work on me while I played for the Celtics. He was the visiting team trainer at the Garden before NBA teams could afford to bring their own man on the road. It killed him to work for the "bad" guys, but he let me sneak up to his clinic where he got me ready for all the big games.

He was so good at his work, in fact, that his massages put me to sleep nearly every time. That could be a problem, and quite often my teammates needled me. They told me that once, after I had fallen asleep on Jock's table, Walter Brown walked into the room and offered me a raise, but I never answered Walter and he walked out, leaving me poorer.

Jock was one of those enthusiastic types that is all too rare in sports and life. There were no half-way measures with Jock, and through the years his enthusiasm infected all of us on the Celtics.

That did not preclude our needling him, however. We'd get him aside before the big games and suggest that he tape the ankles of Elgin Baylor or Oscar Robinson, the league's big stars, together.

"Not too tight so they notice, Jock," we'd say. "Just tight enough."

"'AAaaggghh!" he'd answer. "That would be against the r-r-rules." Then he'd pause. "But if I tied the ankles together loosely, do you think Elgin and Oscar would know something was fishy?"

## Will Cloney
## Director of Boston Marathon

I'm not sure how long I've known Jock Semple; our friendship endured for some five decades. Perhaps survived would be a better word, because life with Jock was not one smooth voyage. It was wind and rain and snow and sleet, but in the end there was always sunshine.

My first fleeting recollections are of Jock as a better than average runner—good enough to be in the first ten in Boston—and good enough for dozens of gold medals, silver cups, plaques, shields and what not from hundreds of shorter races.

He was always a sportswriter's dream, although frequently an interpreter was sorely needed. Jock always talked as if he just landed from Scotland, but if a listener bent an acute ear and paid full attention, Jock became reasonably understandable. Of course that depended, for around marathon time Jock became almost apoplectic. His language defied translation, which was probably a good thing because it would have been unprintable anyway.

"We have formed a reasonably good marathon team: Jock the Skyrocket and Cloney the Diplomat."

We sort of fell into this marathon business together. In 1946, the late Walter Brown (the world's most amateur professional) talked me into taking over the famous BAA indoor track meet. With the big meet came a school meet and the marathon. At that time the marathon was just a fun event, simple to administer, with fields of a few hundred. How things have changed! The meets succumbed to economic pressure, but the marathon grew and grew, and now it's a year-round headache.

At the time, clerical duties were handled by Tom Kanaly, secretary of the BAA and the Boston Garden. But when Tom died shortly thereafter, Jock sort of eased in as the man in charge of entries. For a few years this was not a difficult task, but as the fields increased, so did the paperwork. Jock kept entries on top of his desk, in his desk drawers, in his waste basket, and I think he might even have stashed a few away in his "whirrrllpool." Enter Cloney, striving for emotional control as a search failed to uncover some important communication, some vital entry—although it invariably turned up the day before the race.

Our first major encounter with international fame, or notoriety, came with the much publicized Kathrine Switzer affair. Everyone knows the details, but I will try to set the record straight. Jock and I were both riding the press bus when Kathrine was discovered. I hopped out of the bus and approached her with the thought of removing the offending official number from her gray sweat suit. As I did, a huge runner moved in. Showing remarkably good sense, or at least a thought of self-preservation, I retreated to the bus, passing an irate Jock on the way. Jock kept going, tried to grab the number, and promptly got the treatment from Kathrine's muscular escort.

One enterprising photographer caught me in the act and the picture appeared on the first sports page of the *New York Times*. As a vice president of a stuffy investment company, I really didn't need that kind of publicity (as I was informed caustically by the chairman of the firm the next morning). The picture of Jock got much greater distribution, thank goodness!

There was nothing disingenuous about Jock. He said what he thought, no matter who was around. In his emporium of sweat, everybody was equal. It's funny what nakedness will do. Jock could have a Ph.D. spread out on one table, a hockey player on another, a truck driver in the whirlpool, and a high school runner in the shower. They were all the same to him: tired muscles to knead, stiff necks to crack, deep pains to test the diathermy machine. Jock kept up a steady stream of chatter about the state of the Bruins, the Celtics, and the world, pausing now and then to vent his wrath on the "idiots" who called. His telephone manners did not qualify him for a job in public relations.

I've often been vexed at Jock, seldom angry. But on one occasion I think I would have killed him if I'd had a gun. It was at one of the track meets, and Jock was doing his favorite chore: turning the lap cards to tell runners how many laps were left. Somehow Jock got so excited during a 600-yard run that he fouled up the cards and what should have been a great race turned into a fiasco.

Jock had to go out of his way for that one because the six hundred has three laps and 180 yards. Three laps, three cards! Should be as easy as 3-2-1? Right? Not that night.

But for every harrowing experience, every exasperation, there were dozens of compensating virtues in our relationship. Jock. and Tony Nota, another key Boston Garden employee, would do anything, anytime, to help the BAA. As official airport greeter, Jock was known to hundreds of foreign athletes who came to Boston to fulfill a lifelong ambition to run the marathon. On occasion, he found them lodging, an interpreter—anything they need to prepare them for the race.

Jock was the essence of the Boston Athletic Association. He was primarily responsible for keeping the BAA running team together after the death of Walter Brown. He died a little each time one of his athletes defected to another club. But he didn't carry a grudge. Instead, he ministered to anyone when they needed help.

His fees were ridiculous, nonexistent in many instances. "Who needs money at my stage in life?" he often asked. Jock didn't have to worry. He would have been a millionaire if kind thoughts and affection could be translated into dollars.

## Bobby Orr
### Boston Bruin Hockey Hall of Famer

What more can I say about Jock Semple that hasn't already been said? He yelled a lot. And we all loved him.

# Winners of
# the Boston Marathon

## Men's Open

| Year | Athlete | Country/State | Time |
|------|---------|---------------|------|
| 1897 | John J. McDermott | United States (NY) | 2:55:10 |
| 1898 | Ronald J. MacDonald | Canada | 2:42:00 |
| 1899 | Lawrence Brignolia | United States (MA) | 2:54:38 |
| 1900 | John "Jack" Caffery | Canada | 2:39:44 |
| 1901 | John "Jack" Caffery (2nd victory) | Canada | 2:29:23 |
| 1902 | Sammy Mellor | United States (NY) | 2:43:12 |
| 1903 | John Lorden | United States (MA) | 2:41:29 |
| 1904 | Michael Spring | United States (NY) | 2:38:04 |
| 1905 | Frederick Lorz | United States (NY) | 2:38:25 |
| 1906 | Tim Ford | United States (MA) | 2:45:45 |
| 1907 | Thomas Longboat | Canada | 2:24:24 |
| 1908 | Thomas Morrissey | United States (NY) | 2:25:43 |
| 1909 | Henri Renaud | United States (NH) | 2:53:36 |
| 1910 | Fred Cameron | Canada | 2:28:52 |
| 1911 | Clarence DeMar | United States (MA) | 2:21:39 |
| 1912 | Michael J. Ryan | United States (NY) | 2:21:18 |
| 1913 | Fritz Carlson | United States (MN) | 2:25:14 |
| 1914 | James Duffy | Canada | 2:25:14 |
| 1915 | Édouard Fabre | Canada | 2:31:41 |
| 1916 | Arthur Roth | United States (MA) | 2:27:16 |
| 1917 | Bill Kennedy | United States (NY) | 2:28:37 |
| 1918 | Camp Devens relay team[3] (Race was relay for 10-man military teams) | United States (MA) | 2:29:53 |
| 1919 | Carl Linder | United States (MA) | 2:29:13 |
| 1920 | Peter Trivoulides | United States (NY) | 2:29:31 |
| 1921 | Frank Zuna | United States (NY) | 2:18:57 |
| 1922 | Clarence DeMar (2nd victory) | United States (MA) | 2:18:10 |

| | | | |
|---|---|---|---|
| 1923 | Clarence DeMar (3rd victory) | United States (MA) | 2:23:47 |
| 1924 | Clarence DeMar (4th victory) | United States (MA) | 2:29:40 |
| 1925 | Charles Mellor | United States (IL) | 2:33:00 |
| 1926 | Johnny Miles | Canada | 2:25:40 |
| 1927 | Clarence DeMar (5th victory) | United States (MA) | 2:40:22 |
| 1928 | Clarence DeMar (6th victory) | United States (MA) | 2:37:07 |
| 1929 | Johnny Miles (2nd victory) | Canada | 2:33:08 |
| 1930 | Clarence DeMar (7th victory) | United States (MA) | 2:34:48 |
| 1931 | James Henigan | United States (MA) | 2:46:45 |
| 1932 | Paul de Bruyn | Germany | 2:33:36 |
| 1933 | Leslie S. Pawson | United States (RI) | 2:31:01 |
| 1934 | Dave Komonen | Canada | 2:32:53 |
| 1935 | John A. Kelley | United States (MA) | 2:32:07 |
| 1936 | Ellison Brown | United States (RI) | 2:33:40 |
| 1937 | Walter Young | Canada | 2:33:20 |
| 1938 | Leslie S. Pawson (2nd victory) | United States (RI) | 2:35:34 |
| 1939 | Ellison Brown (2nd victory) | United States (RI) | 2:28:51 |
| 1940 | Gérard Côté | Canada | 2:28:28 |
| 1941 | Leslie S. Pawson (3rd victory) | United States (RI) | 2:30:38 |
| 1942 | Joe Smith | United States (MA) | 2:26:51 |
| 1943 | Gérard Côté (2nd victory) | Canada | 2:28:25 |
| 1944 | Gérard Côté (3rd victory) | Canada | 2:31:50 |
| 1945 | John A. Kelley (2nd victory) | United States (MA) | 2:30:40 |

| 1946 | Stylianos Kyriakides (Only Greek to ever win the marathon) | Greece | 2:29:27 |
|------|------------------------------------------------------------|--------|---------|
| 1947 | Suh Yun-bok | South Korea | 2:25:39 |
| 1948 | Gérard Côté (4th victory) | Canada | 2:31:02 |
| 1949 | Gösta Leandersson | Sweden | 2:31:50 |
| 1950 | Ham Kee-Yong | South Korea | 2:32:39 |
| 1951 | Shigeki Tanaka | Japan | 2:27:45 |
| 1952 | Doroteo Flores (Only Guatemalan to ever win the marathon) | Guatemala | 2:31:53 |
| 1953 | Keizo Yamada | Japan | 2:18:51 |
| 1954 | Veikko Karvonen | Finland | 2:20:39 |
| 1955 | Hideo Hamamura | Japan | 2:18:22 |
| 1956 | Antti Viskari | Finland | 2:14:14 |
| 1957 | John J. Kelley | United States (CT) | 2:20:05 |
| 1958 | Franjo Mihalić | Yugoslavia | 2:25:54 |
| 1959 | Eino Oksanen | Finland | 2:22:42 |
| 1960 | Paavo Kotila | Finland | 2:20:54 |
| 1961 | Eino Oksanen (2nd victory) | Finland | 2:23:39 |
| 1962 | Eino Oksanen (3rd victory) | Finland | 2:23:48 |
| 1963 | Aurèle Vandendriessche | Belgium | 2:18:58 |
| 1964 | Aurèle Vandendriessche (2nd victory) | Belgium | 2:19:59 |
| 1965 | Morio Shigematsu | Japan | 2:16:33 |
| 1966 | Kenji Kimihara | Japan | 2:17:11 |
| 1967 | Dave McKenzie | New Zealand | 2:15:45 |
| 1968 | Amby Burfoot | United States (CT) | 2:22:17 |
| 1969 | Yoshiaki Unetani | Japan | 2:13:49 |
| 1970 | Ron Hill | United Kingdom | 2:10:30 |
| 1971 | Álvaro Mejía | Colombia | 2:18:45 |
| 1972 | Olavi Suomalainen | Finland | 2:15:39 |
| 1973 | Jon Anderson | United States (OR) | 2:16:03 |
| 1974 | Neil Cusack | Ireland | 2:13:39 |

| 1975 | Bill Rodgers | United States (MA) | 2:09:55 |
| 1976 | Jack Fultz | United States (VA) | 2:20:19 |
| 1977 | Jerome Drayton | Canada | 2:14:46 |
| 1978 | Bill Rodgers (2nd victory) | United States (MA) | 2:10:13 |
| 1979 | Bill Rodgers (3rd victory) | United States (MA) | 2:09:27 |
| 1980 | Bill Rodgers (4th victory) | United States (MA) | 2:12:11 |
| 1981 | Toshihiko Seko | Japan | 2:09:26 |
| 1982 | Alberto Salazar | United States (MA) | 2:08:52 |
| 1983 | Greg Meyer | United States (MI) | 2:09:00 |
| 1984 | Geoff Smith | United Kingdom | 2:10:34 |
| 1985 | Geoff Smith (2nd victory) | United Kingdom | 2:14:05 |
| 1986 | Robert de Castella | Australia | 2:07:51 |
| 1987 | Toshihiko Seko (2nd victory) | Japan | 2:11:50 |
| 1988 | Ibrahim Hussein | Kenya | 2:08:43 |
| 1989 | Abebe Mekonnen | Ethiopia | 2:09:06 |
| 1990 | Gelindo Bordin | Italy | 2:08:19 |
| 1991 | Ibrahim Hussein (2nd victory) | Kenya | 2:11:06 |
| 1992 | Ibrahim Hussein (3rd victory) | Kenya | 2:08:14 |
| 1993 | Cosmas Ndeti | Kenya | 2:09:33 |
| 1994 | Cosmas Ndeti (2nd victory) | Kenya | 2:07:15 |
| 1995 | Cosmas Ndeti (3rd victory) | Kenya | 2:09:22 |
| 1996 | Moses Tanui | Kenya | 2:09:15 |
| 1997 | Lameck Aguta | Kenya | 2:10:34 |
| 1998 | Moses Tanui (2nd victory) | Kenya | 2:07:34 |
| 1999 | Joseph Chebet | Kenya | 2:09:52 |

| | | | |
|---|---|---|---|
| 2000 | Elijah Lagat | Kenya | 2:09:47 |
| 2001 | Lee Bong-Ju | South Korea | 2:09:43 |
| 2002 | Rodgers Rop | Kenya | 2:09:02 |
| 2003 | Robert Kipkoech Cheruiyot | Kenya | 2:10:11 |
| 2004 | Timothy Cherigat | Kenya | 2:10:37 |
| 2005 | Hailu Negussie | Ethiopia | 2:11:44 |
| 2006 | Robert Kipkoech Cheruiyot (2nd victory) | Kenya | 2:07:14 |
| 2007 | Robert Kipkoech Cheruiyot (3rd victory) | Kenya | 2:14:13 |
| 2008 | Robert Kipkoech Cheruiyot (4th victory) | Kenya | 2:07:45 |
| 2009 | Deriba Merga | Ethiopia | 2:08:42 |
| 2010 | Robert Kiprono Cheruiyot | Kenya | 2:05:52 |
| 2011 | Geoffrey Mutai | Kenya | 2:03:02 |
| 2012 | Wesley Korir | Kenya | 2:12:40 |
| 2013 | Lelisa Desisa Benti | Ethiopia | 2:10:22 |
| 2014 | Meb Keflezighi (First American win since 1983) | United States (CA) | 2:08:37 |
| 2015 | Lelisa Desisa Benti (2nd victory) | Ethiopia | 2:09:17 |
| 2016 | Lemi Berhanu Hayle | Ethiopia | 2:12:45 |

## Women's Open

| Year | Athlete | Country/State | Time |
|---|---|---|---|
| 1966 | Bobbi Gibb (unsanctioned) [4] | United States (MA) | 3:21:40 |
| 1967 | Bobbi Gibb (unsanctioned) 2nd victory [4] | United States (CA) | 3:27:17 |
| 1968 | Bobbi Gibb (unsanctioned) 3rd victory [4] | United States (CA) | 3:30:00 |
| 1969 | Sara Mae Berman (unsanctioned) [4] | United States (MA) | 3:22:46 |
| 1970 | Sara Mae Berman (unsanctioned) 2nd victory [4] | United States (MA) | 3:05:07 |

| 1971 | Sara Mae Berman (unsanctioned) 3rd victory [4] | United States (MA) | 3:08:30 |
|------|------|------|------|
| 1972 | Nina Kuscsik (First year women were officially sanctioned) | United States (NY) | 3:10:26 |
| 1973 | Jacqueline Hansen | United States (CA) | 3:05:59 |
| 1974 | Miki Gorman | United States (CA) | 2:47:11 |
| 1975 | Liane Winter | West Germany | 2:42:24 |
| 1976 | Kim Merritt | United States (WI) | 2:47:10 |
| 1977 | Miki Gorman (2nd victory) | United States (CA) | 2:48:33 |
| 1978 | Gayle Barron | United States (GA) | 2:44:52 |
| 1979 | Joan Benoit | United States (ME) | 2:35:15 |
| 1980 | Jacqueline Gareau | Canada | 2:34:28 [5] |
| 1981 | Allison Roe | New Zealand | 2:26:46 |
| 1982 | Charlotte Teske | West Germany | 2:29:33 |
| 1983 | Joan Benoit (2nd victory) | United States (ME) | 2:22:43 |
| 1984 | Lorraine Moller | New Zealand | 2:29:28 |
| 1985 | Lisa Larsen Weidenbach | United States (MI) | 2:34.06 |
| 1986 | Ingrid Kristiansen | Norway | 2:24:55 |
| 1987 | Rosa Mota | Portugal | 2:25:21 |
| 1988 | Rosa Mota (2nd victory) | Portugal | 2:24:30 |
| 1989 | Ingrid Kristiansen (2nd victory) | Norway | 2:24:33 |
| 1990 | Rosa Mota (3rd victory) | Portugal | 2:25:24 |
| 1991 | Wanda Panfil | Poland | 2:24:18 |
| 1992 | Olga Markova | Russia | 2:23:43 |
| 1993 | Olga Markova (2nd victory) | Russia | 2:25:27 |
| 1994 | Uta Pippig | Germany | 2:21:45 |
| 1995 | Uta Pippig | Germany | 2:25:11 |

|      | (2nd victory) | | |
|------|---------------|---------|---------|
| 1996 | Uta Pippig (3rd victory) | Germany | 2:27:12 |
| 1997 | Fatuma Roba | Ethiopia | 2:26:23 |
| 1998 | Fatuma Roba (2nd victory) | Ethiopia | 2:23:21 |
| 1999 | Fatuma Roba (3rd victory) | Ethiopia | 2:23:25 |
| 2000 | Catherine Ndereba | Kenya | 2:26:11 |
| 2001 | Catherine Ndereba (2nd victory) | Kenya | 2:23:53 |
| 2002 | Margaret Okayo | Kenya | 2:20:43 |
| 2003 | Svetlana Zakharova | Russia | 2:25:19 |
| 2004 | Catherine Ndereba (3rd victory) | Kenya | 2:24:27 |
| 2005 | Catherine Ndereba (4th victory) | Kenya | 2:25:12 |
| 2006 | Rita Jeptoo | Kenya | 2:23:38 |
| 2007 | Lidiya Grigoryeva | Russia | 2:29:18 |
| 2008 | Dire Tune (2 seconds ahead of 2nd-place finisher) | Ethiopia | 2:25:25 |
| 2009 | Salina Kosgei (1 second ahead of 2nd-place finisher) | Kenya | 2:32:16 |
| 2010 | Teyba Erkesso (3 seconds ahead of 2nd-place finisher) | Ethiopia | 2:26:11 |
| 2011 | Caroline Kilel (2 seconds ahead of 2nd-place finisher) | Kenya | 2:22:36 |
| 2012 | Sharon Cherop (2 seconds ahead of 2nd-place finisher) | Kenya | 2:31:50 |
| 2013 | Rita Jeptoo (2nd victory) | Kenya | 2:26:25 |
| 2014 | Rita Jeptoo (3rd victory) | Kenya | 2:18:57 |
| 2015 | Caroline Rotich | Kenya | 2:24:55 |
| 2016 | Atsede Baysa | Ethiopia | 2:29:19 |

## Men's Wheelchair

| Year | Athlete | Country/State | Time |
|------|---------|---------------|------|
| 1975 | Robert Hall | United States (MA) | 2:58:00 |
| 1976 | none | | |
| 1977 | Robert Hall (2nd victory) | United States (MA) | 2:40:10 |
| 1978 | George Murray | United States (FL) | 2:26:57 |
| 1979 | Ken Archer | United States (OH) | 2:38:59 |
| 1980 | Curt Brinkman | United States (UT) | 1:55:00 |
| 1981 | Jim Martinson | United States (WA) | 2:00:41 |
| 1982 | Jim Knaub | United States (CA) | 1:51:31 |
| 1983 | Jim Knaub (2nd victory) | United States (CA) | 1:47:10 |
| 1984 | André Viger | Canada | 2:05:20 |
| 1985 | George Murray (2nd victory) | United States (FL) | 1:45:34 |
| 1986 | André Viger (2nd victory) | Canada | 1:43:25 |
| 1987 | André Viger (3rd victory) | Canada | 1:55:42 |
| 1988 | Mustapha Badid | France | 1:43:19 |
| 1989 | Philippe Couprie | France | 1:36:04 |
| 1990 | Mustapha Badid (2nd victory) | France | 1:29:53 |
| 1991 | Jim Knaub (3rd victory) | United States (CA) | 1:30:44 |
| 1992 | Jim Knaub (4th victory) | United States (CA) | 1:26:28 |
| 1993 | Jim Knaub (5th victory) | United States (CA) | 1:22:17 |
| 1994 | Heinz Frei | Switzerland | 1:21:23 |
| 1995 | Franz Nietlispach | Switzerland | 1:25:59 |
| 1996 | Heinz Frei (2nd victory) | Switzerland | 1:30:14 |

| | | | |
|---|---|---|---|
| 1997 | Franz Nietlispach (2nd victory) | Switzerland | 1:28:14 |
| 1998 | Franz Nietlispach (3rd victory) | Switzerland | 1:21:52 |
| 1999 | Franz Nietlispach (4th victory) | Switzerland | 1:21:36 |
| 2000 | Franz Nietlispach (5th victory) | Switzerland | 1:33:32 |
| 2001 | Ernst van Dyk | South Africa | 1:25:12 |
| 2002 | Ernst van Dyk (2nd victory) | South Africa | 1:23:19 |
| 2003 | Ernst van Dyk (3rd victory) | South Africa | 1:28:32 |
| 2004 | Ernst van Dyk (4th victory) | South Africa | 1:18:27 |
| 2005 | Ernst van Dyk (5th victory) | South Africa | 1:24:11 |
| 2006 | Ernst van Dyk (6th victory) | South Africa | 1:25:29 |
| 2007 | Masazumi Soejima | Japan | 1:29:16 |
| 2008 | Ernst van Dyk (7th victory) | South Africa | 1:26:49 |
| 2009 | Ernst van Dyk (8th victory) | South Africa | 1:33:29 |
| 2010 | Ernst van Dyk (9th victory) | South Africa | 1:26:53 |
| 2011 | Masazumi Soejima (2nd victory) | Japan | 1:18:50 |
| 2012 | Joshua Cassidy | Canada | 1:18:25 |
| 2013 | Hiroyuki Yamamoto | Japan | 1:25:33 |
| 2014 | Ernst van Dyk (10th victory) | South Africa | 1:20:36 |
| 2015 | Marcel Hug | Switzerland | 1:29:53 |
| 2016 | Marcel Hug (2nd victory) | Switzerland | 1:24:01 |

**Women's Wheelchair**

| Year | Athlete | Country/State | Time |
|------|---------|---------------|------|
| 1977 | Sharon Rahn | United States (IL) | 3:48:51 |
| 1978 | Susan Shapiro | United States (CA) | 3:52:35 |
| 1979 | Sheryl Bair | United States (CA) | 3:27:56 |
| 1980 | Sharon Limpert | United States (MN) | 2:49:04 |
| 1981 | Candace Cable-Brookes | United States (NV) | 2:38:41 |
| 1982 | Candace Cable-Brookes (2nd victory) | United States (NV) | 2:12:43 |
| 1983 | Sherry Ramsey | United States (CO) | 2:27:07 |
| 1984 | Sherry Ramsey (2nd victory) | United States (CO) | 2:56:51 |
| 1985 | Candace Cable-Brookes (3rd victory) | United States (CA) | 2:05:26 |
| 1986 | Candace Cable-Brookes (4th victory) | United States (CA) | 2:09:28 |
| 1987 | Candace Cable-Brookes (5th victory) | United States (CA) | 2:19:55 |
| 1988 | Candace Cable-Brookes (6th victory) | United States (CA) | 2:10:44 |
| 1989 | Connie Hansen | Denmark | 1:50:06 |
| 1990 | Jean Driscoll | United States (IL) | 1:43:17 |
| 1991 | Jean Driscoll (2nd victory) | United States (IL) | 1:42:42 |
| 1992 | Jean Driscoll (3rd victory) | United States (IL) | 1:36:52 |
| 1993 | Jean Driscoll (4th victory) | United States (IL) | 1:34:50 |
| 1994 | Jean Driscoll (5th victory) | United States (IL) | 1:34:22 |
| 1995 | Jean Driscoll (6th victory) | United States (IL) | 1:40:42 |
| 1996 | Jean Driscoll (7th victory) | United States (IL) | 1:52:56 |

| 1997 | Louise Sauvage | Australia | 1:54:28 |
| 1998 | Louise Sauvage (2nd victory) | Australia | 1:41:19 |
| 1999 | Louise Sauvage (3rd victory) | Australia | 1:42:23 |
| 2000 | Jean Driscoll (8th victory) | United States (IL) | 2:00:52 |
| 2001 | Louise Sauvage (4th victory) | Australia | 1:53:54 |
| 2002 | Edith Hunkeler | Switzerland | 1:45:57 |
| 2003 | Christina Ripp | United States (IL) | 1:54:47 |
| 2004 | Cheri Blauwet | United States (CA) | 1:39:53 |
| 2005 | Cheri Blauwet (2nd victory) | United States (CA) | 1:47:45 |
| 2006 | Edith Hunkeler (2nd victory) | Switzerland | 1:43:42 |
| 2007 | Wakako Tsuchida | Japan | 1:53:30 |
| 2008 | Wakako Tsuchida (2nd victory) | Japan | 1:48:32 |
| 2009 | Wakako Tsuchida (3rd victory) | Japan | 1:54:37 |
| 2010 | Wakako Tsuchida (4th victory) | Japan | 1:43:32 |
| 2011 | Wakako Tsuchida (5th victory) | Japan | 1:34:06 |
| 2012 | Shirley Reilly | United States (AZ) | 1:37:36 |
| 2013 | Tatyana McFadden | United States (MD) | 1:45:25 |
| 2014 | Tatyana McFadden (2nd victory) | United States (MD) | 1:35:06 |
| 2015 | Tatyana McFadden (3rd victory) | United States (MD) | 1:52:54 |
| 2016 | Tatyana McFadden (4th victory) | United States (MD) | 1:42:16 |

## Victories by Nationality

| Country | Men's Open | Women's Open | Men's Wheelchair | Women's Wheelchair | Total |
|---|---|---|---|---|---|
| United States | 45 | 15 | 12 | 28 | 100 |
| Kenya | 20 | 12 | 0 | 0 | 32 |
| Canada | 16 | 1 | 4 | 0 | 21 |
| Japan | 8 | 0 | 3 | 5 | 16 |
| Switzerland | 0 | 0 | 9 | 2 | 11 |
| Ethiopia | 6 | 5 | 0 | 0 | 11 |
| South Africa | 0 | 0 | 10 | 0 | 10 |
| Finland | 7 | 0 | 0 | 0 | 7 |
| Germany | 1 | 5[6] | 0 | 0 | 6 |
| Australia | 1 | 0 | 0 | 4 | 5 |
| Russia | 0 | 4 | 0 | 0 | 4 |
| France | 0 | 0 | 3 | 0 | 3 |
| New Zealand | 1 | 2 | 0 | 0 | 3 |
| Portugal | 0 | 3 | 0 | 0 | 3 |
| South Korea | 3 | 0 | 0 | 0 | 3 |
| UK | 3 | 0 | 0 | 0 | 3 |
| Belgium | 2 | 0 | 0 | 0 | 2 |
| Norway | 0 | 2 | 0 | 0 | 2 |
| Colombia | 1 | 0 | 0 | 0 | 1 |
| Denmark | 0 | 0 | 0 | 1 | 1 |
| Greece | 1 | 0 | 0 | 0 | 1 |
| Guatemala | 1 | 0 | 0 | 0 | 1 |
| Ireland | 1 | 0 | 0 | 0 | 1 |
| Italy | 1 | 0 | 0 | 0 | 1 |
| Poland | 0 | 1 | 0 | 0 | 1 |
| Sweden | 1 | 0 | 0 | 0 | 1 |
| Yugoslavia | 1 | 0 | 0 | 0 | 1 |

1. *"Mutai wins Boston in world-record time: Kilel edges American in women's race."* *Boston Herald*, Associated Press. April 18, 2011.

2. May, Peter (April 18, 2011). *"Kenya's Mutai Wins Boston in 2:03:02."* *The New York Times.*

3. Due to American involvement in World War I, the 1918 race was run as a ten-man relay for teams from military bases across the United States. The winner was the team from Camp Devens, Massachusetts.

4. The first six victories in the women's open division were unofficial, until the race was officially recognized in 1996.

5. Another runner, Rosie Ruiz, was originally declared the winner of the 1980 marathon. When it was determined that she cheated, Gareau was named the winner.

6. This includes two victories by West German athletes during the Cold War.

# About the Authors

## Tom Murphy

Tom Murphy had just earned his MFA in Creative Writing at the University of British Columbia in Vancouver in 1979, following several years teaching in Boston schools, when Jock Semple asked Tom to write his life story. The book was published to positive reviews in the *New York Times* and other media in 1982. In 2006 Tom wrote *Reclaiming the Sky*, a story about the courageous aviation workers in New York, Boston and Washington, DC on 9/11. Fordham University invited Tom to establish the Human Resiliency Institute

 at Fordham in New York, where Tom created Edge4Vets to help veterans returning from the wars in Iraq and Afghanistan tap their resiliency strengths to get jobs. In 2014 after his wife, Barb, a Boston Marathon runner, passed away from non-smoker's lung cancer, Tom created Barb's Beer to support efforts to find a cure for non-smoker's lung cancer. See more at barbsbeer.org.

## John J. Kelley

John J. Kelley, often called Johnny Kelley "the Younger" to distinguish him from John A. Kelley "the Elder," no relation, was America's premier marathon runner during the 1950s and 60s. Twice, Johnny competed in the Olympics, in 1956 and 60. In 1957 he won the Boston Marathon and finished second on five other occasions.

He won the American national marathon championship eight times in a row, a record. Jock served not only as Johnny's trainer, but also as his "father/confessor," as Johnny described their relationship. In addition to being an outstanding runner, Johnny was a talented writer and for decades contributed to newspapers and running magazines in his native Mystic, Connecticut, where he taught high school English and raised three daughters with his wife, Jessie: Julia, Kathleen, and Eileen. Johnny offered finely drawn portraits of Jock, and also of the road runners of Jock's era. In the "Jock book" he captures with great insight the lives of these pioneers of American marathon running, called plodders, who by the fifties were giving way to the younger college runners, epitomized by Johnny and the legion of American champions, including Bill Rodgers, Amby Burfoot, and others who followed. Johnny passed away in 2011 from lung cancer.

Left to right: John J. Kelley, Jock Semple, and Tom Murphy.